# Selling Your Art

*by*

**Douglas Ready**

*Selling Your Art*

by

**Douglas Ready**

*Visit online at* **www.douglasready.com.**

*To my wonderful, beautiful life Mona who makes every day extraordinary, and to the memory of her mother and the second joy of my life Maxine Dyson.*

**Selling Your Art**

### Introduction:  The Artist & the Illustrator

There are only two ways to earn money as an artist.

The first is to independently create an image and find someone with the desire and the means to purchase that image. The second is to find someone with the desire and means to enlist your skills to generate an image that reflects their own imagination.  In the first scenario, the artist has sold a product. In the second, the artist has sold a service resulting in the creation of a product.

One who creates work designed from his own internal mechanisms is generally referred to as an Artist.  One who creates work designed to illuminate an idea generated by someone other than the artist is generally referred to as an Illustrator.  These descriptors are used to suggest a functional direction of purpose and nothing more.  Both functions require a requisite amount of artistic talent and skill and inherent creativity.  Both the Artist and the Illustrator may well wind up producing the same kind of work, applying the same kind of skills and utilizing the same kind of working materials. Regardless of the arena in which one chooses to apply those skills, it is reasonable to consider both artists.

As artists we are often presented with the notion that seriously attempting to generate a monetary return from what we produce is somehow beneath us, that exchanging our creative endeavors for financial gain somehow minimizes our accomplishments.  Only in the creative sphere, and for some unfathomable reason especially the arena reserved for those of us who drag drawing implements across blank surfaces, is this concept given any serious consideration.  Suggest to an automobile manufacturer or a pharmaceutical concern or even a movie production studio that their efforts are best geared toward the production of altruistic aesthetics--that they should profit from their labors only in a purely artistic sense--and they'll laugh your butt right off their respective premises.

And rightly so.

Nobody becomes an artist just to make money. If financial return is the primary goal, there are a variety of methods guaranteed to help one achieve that end with a great deal less headache and less heartache, not to mention less aggravation. It is reasonable, however, to not only expect but also require that one's professional efforts consistently produce enough return to allow the regular acquisition of groceries and the disbursement of monies designated for rent, clothing, utilities and the occasional romantic foray.

The Oxford American Dictionary defines *professional* as doing a certain kind of work as a full-time occupation or to make a living or for payment. If your choice is to apply your hard-learned skills to the production of artistic projects solely for aesthetic satisfaction I salute your heartfelt personal conviction and wish you the best of luck in securing a day-job that will hopefully not completely drain whatever creative energy could have been applied to the creation of artwork that might have enlightened or at least entertained a healthy-sized chunk of your fellow man and earned you a reasonable financial return to boot.

If on the other hand you've come to understand that Art with a capital A is a term that for working purposes is probably best left to the discretional consideration of others and that exchanging your own creative endeavors for cold, hard cash by no means diminishes your work's significance--in fact may actually enhance your work's influence--then the time has come to take a good look at your abilities and potential and to formally structure a Professional Career.

You do the work because you enjoy doing the work. Getting paid for the work allows you to continue doing the work. It's that simple. The romantic myth of the struggling artist tucked into a filthy garret devouring yesterday's leftover and slightly molded kidney beans so he can save whatever precious few dollars he's been able to hoard to just about afford one more piece of canvas to cover with crusted paint is just that--a myth. That guy's career prospects undoubtedly include selling shoes at the mall, smug in the knowledge that he refused to sell-out.

Selling-out isn't the issue. The issue is selling, period.

## Creating and Selling Art is a Job

A professional artist understands that artistic creation, if it is to be more than an exercise in a solitary and even self-congratulatory pursuit, must be approached on a daily basis as an endeavor designed to enhance the monetary standing of the participant.

In other words, it's a job.

The artist must actively endeavor to acquire those skills not only imperative to producing the imagery so dearly important to him, but also the skills necessary to assure that the finished product is adequately displayed to a customer base. Many of us spend years learning the subtleties of applying inks and colors, but neglect--or even outright refuse--to learn the basic principles of marketing and sales, feeling that embracing these particular abilities is somehow beneath us, somehow taints our creative purity. The simple truth is that the artist who refuses to embrace the principles of basic marketing and learn elementary sales techniques seriously--perhaps terminally--undermines the possibility of finding the exposure necessary to build a dependable collector list or customer base.

The artist also realizes that building a career is a daily pursuit.

## Inventory Your Skills

The artist must be realistic about the achievement of his objective. He must make certain he has acquired the necessary skills he needs to be successful, and if not the artist must be prepared to acquire those skills, both the artistic and the non-artistic.

There are certainly instances when an unqualified, less than competent creative hack has somehow managed to stumble into something that offers an incredible financial return on what little he has to offer. More often, success occurs when a practiced professional has taken the time to properly learn the application of the skills he's acquired and is recognized for his accomplishment.

**Itemize Your Attitude**

Ego is the biggest hurdle the working artist must overcome if he is to have any chance of lasting success.

A certain pride in one's abilities and the willingness to acknowledge that the work produced is truly viable and valuable is essential to the artist's survival, but the blind refusal to identify areas of less than stellar conception and execution and the unwillingness to engage in an improvement strategy to correct the problem will mark the artist as something other than professional and guarantee a lifetime of pursuing what one can only hope will remain a satisfying hobby.

The artist must learn to separate himself emotionally from the work he produces, if only for a period of time long enough to recognize that which must be improved. And, the artist must learn to recognize when the required amount of improvement is so immense that he might actually be better off pursuing other venues.

For an artist, there is no vision until that vision is shared. An unshared vision is merely a concept, lines on paper or paint on canvas that will never enlighten, entice or entertain. Continuous creation is paramount, if for no other reason the continuous application of skill is the only method of developing a truly unique and original personal style--essential if the artist is to not only survive, but thrive.

### The Importance of a Business Plan

The single factor separating the professional artist from the hobbyist is the intent to sell--intent, not desire. The professional structures his work schedule and his output to produce a required minimum amount of imagery to allow appropriate presentation to potential buyers, whether that presentation is to be directed toward the private collector or toward the art director whose concerns are wholly commercial.

The artist must consider the possibilities inherent in his particular abilities and decide in what directions he will focus his creative efforts. Whether the artist decides to produce stand-alone pieces or whether he decides to pursue some faction of the commercial market, he will need to focus promotional efforts on his areas of choice.

Commercial assignments will most certainly not find their way to his studio unless they are directed there. Wall space to hang original art won't be revealed unless those who manage the blank space are aware of the artist's ability and availability. The artist must first identify those areas in which his skills suggest some viability, then target those areas he has an interest in pursuing. A preliminary business plan is nothing more than a written directive planning the creation and submission of work to various potential markets. The plan will necessarily include a time frame for completion of the different factions so the artist may gauge his performance.

### Function, Production, Promotion and Perception

There are many factors the artist cannot control in his pursuit of financial solvency, especially in the beginning days of his career. The artist must learn to focus on those areas that can be controlled, and control them to the best of his ability.

**Function** is directly controllable. The artist is the one who determines that he will indeed spend a specified amount of time at the drawing board or easel, or devote a particular block of time to improving a specific skill.

**Production** is directly controllable. The artist is the one who sets production deadlines, even if in the early stages of his career the deadlines are capricious.

**Promotion** is directly controllable. The successful artist is the one who makes the effort to put his work in front of new prospects, and while there can be no guarantee of a sale there must certainly be a guarantee of a minimum number of presentations if the artist is to find success.

**Perception** is directly controllable. The artist is the one who must constantly reevaluate his skills--and his mindset--to make sure he is truly up to the task of continuously producing a viable product that can be successfully promoted and sold.

Simply put, making a living as an artist comes down to these steps:

**1. Learn your craft and practice it continuously.**

**2. Produce as much work as you possibly can and make sure the artwork that leaves your studio is the best work you can produce. And make sure a *lot* of work leaves your studio.**

**3. Never miss an opportunity for self-promotion. Understand that opportunity is made, not found.**

**4. Repeat Steps One, Two and Three every day, day in and day out for the rest of your professional working life.**

Understand that the mediums you choose to work with

today might not be the mediums that best showcase your abilities, and be open to making adjustments that will eventually serve you better.

Understand that every action will not bring a desired result. Know that rejection from any quarter is a temporary annoyance, nothing more and nothing less.

Review your work, your goals and your plan of action for achievement regularly. Retain what seems to garner a return, reject what doesn't. There are literally hundreds of different pathways to finding success as an artist, and each of them is a valid route so long as you wind up at your chosen destination. If one approach isn't working for you, discard it and try another. And another. And another.

As my grandfather used to say: You can't always get what you want, but you can generally get what you chase.

### The Professional Artist:  Hobby vs. Career

Artists who make a living producing creative work understand one simple truth:

### *Creating and selling art is a job.*

A professional artist is in effect an independent business operation, a manufacturing endeavor concerned with the concept and creation of an artistic product and the marketing and sales of that product.  If the artist lacks the ability to complete a reasonably unique project on a continuing basis, chances are his efforts will blend into the multitude of other proffered creative efforts and become lost in the shuffle, never allowing the gathering of a clientele anxiously awaiting the artist's next work.  Likewise, if the artist refuses to embrace the principles of basic marketing and learn elementary sales technique, chances are his efforts will never find the exposure necessary to build a dependable customer list.

A professional artist is one who has come to understand that exchanging his efforts for monetary compensation in no way, shape or form diminishes the work.  He understands that the emotional aspect of art is best applied during the creation phase of the job and pushed aside if it interferes with the selling phase of the job.

A professional artist understands the working aspects of his job, both functionally and philosophically.  He strives to master those tools and techniques which will result in the creation of projects more likely to endear him to those who might purchase his work.  He recognizes that a job is a continual process, lasting the full day and beginning again the next day, and knows that his job performance requires a critique not only in the area of artistic competence, but also in the  areas of persistence, volume and follow through.

Again, the single factor separating the professional artist from the hobbyist is the intent to sell--intent, not desire. Many a hobbyist spends four hours a week working on a painting he or she hopes might be sold to a friend or neighbor who happens to wander in and see the piece. The professional structures his work schedule and his output to produce a required minimum amount of imagery to allow appropriate presentation to potential buyers, whether that presentation is to be directed toward the private collector or toward an art director whose concerns are wholly commercial.

The professional artist understands that inspiration is a wonderful thing, but that it cannot be depended upon for consistently coherent  suggestion.

### Selling Your Product vs. Selling Your Skills

The division between so-called Fine Art and art produced for Commercial purposes becomes blurrier with each passing day. Artwork originally produced as a stand-alone piece continuously shows up in commercial venues; likewise, artwork originally produced for a specific commercial situation finds its way into venues designed to appeal to the individual collector. A glance at one of the most commercial of all art markets, the comic book publishing industry, quickly verifies this duality for the objet d'art:  original comic book art regularly sells on the collector's market for a higher per page rate than most publishers pay the creators.

It matters less and less whether the art found creation as a stand-alone piece or as a means of communicating specific commercial information. Collectors seem determined to acquire art from both categories and both signed checks result in art hanging on somebody's wall.

The artist who is truly a solitary individual, one who simply lacks the patience required--or just the inclination--to function in a communal creative atmosphere, would do well to avoid commercial commissions. This particular mindset is really the only valid argument for refusing to explore the income possibilities inherent in commercial work.

### Directing Your Career

The artist must consider the possibilities inherent in his particular abilities and decide in what directions he will focus his creative efforts. Regardless of whether the artist decides to produce stand-alone pieces or whether he decides to pursue some faction of the commercial market, he will need to focus promotional efforts on his areas of choice.

In today's splintered marketplace, it is no longer adequate to simply proclaim one's self an artist; one must proclaim not only his talents and abilities, but his intent.

### Maximize the Imagery

In order to realize the fullest potential financial return from his efforts, the artist must always consider the widest spectrum of imagery placement.

Often, a work created as a stand-alone piece has the potential to increase the artist's income not only as a sold original, but also as a print or poster, a greeting card or a collectable plate. The artist must fully explore every possible financial exploitation of the imagery he creates and pursue those options. He should especially pursue those options that offer continuing income in the form of royalties. This is sometimes referred to as residual income and offers possibly the best chance of long-term financial security for the artist.

### Thinking Outside the Box

The goal of financial security is not achieved by a strident change of the artist's interest or focus. As artists, we all have those areas of creation that excite us and our choices of mediums and subject matters are dictated by that excitement.

Financial security is best achieved not by twisting our output to meet the demands of a perceived market, but by allowing ourselves to consider every possible exploitation of the imagery we create.

Exploitation is a word with a somewhat distasteful reputation. I use it only in the context of consideration of possibility, the exploration of different venues in which imagery may be displayed, therefore generating a financial return.

Years ago, an artist friend of mine spend all his working hours producing ink drawings placed firmly within the realm of the sword and sorcery genre. The imagery produced was striking, bold swatches of black ink swirled to form muscular warriors and comely wenches and the occasional mythical beast.

James, dressed in Buccaneer boots and a white flowing Poet's shirt would set up at Street Fairs on weekends. Tall, slender with a tapered goatee, his physical presence worked quite will with the images he'd matted and framed and offered for purchase.

The problem was that the average household isn't really decorated to accommodate black and white renderings of axe-wielding adventurers, no matter how appealing the scantily-clad slave girl tucked into the corner of the picture. People would look and the comments were generally complimentary, but sales were few and far between.

What irritated James more than the lack of sales was a comment heard often across the booth: "Wow! I'd love that on a t-shirt!"

James considered himself a serious artist. Self-taught, his drawing and inking skills were among the best I'd ever encountered. His pictures were mesmerizing.

They just didn't mesh well into anyone's living room.

James took his original art and matted and framed them in pre-cut materials to a finished size of 11" x 14". He sold those packaged originals for $50.

I pointed out that screen printing 25 each of his four most commented-on designs would cost him somewhere in the neighborhood of $250. Selling the shirts at $10 each would bring in $1000, yielding a $750 profit.

And, James would still own the original art.

Eventually, James moved into poster and comic book work. He published a popular series of children's books featuring his own Fluffy, a cat-sized dinosaur. He also became a respected and much sought after producer of Civil War prints.

Along the way, though, James sold some 7500 t-shirts.

## Tools of the Trade

A business license announces to the world that the artist is a professional, not a hobbyist. The license doesn't make you an artist, but it does lend credibility to the concept that you're pursuing a professional career.

A business license also entitles you to a professional discount at art supply shops, picture framers and commercial printers. In some instances the license permits you not to pay sales tax on certain items purchased for use in your business operations.

The license allows you to buy directly from manufacturers and distributors if you're willing to meet their minimum purchase requirements. If your particular working methods dictate use of large quantities of particular supplies, buying direct will save you 50% of the retail price.

You'll need the license to set up at Street Fairs and Festivals.

If you intend to produce product and distribute product--greeting cards, posters, prints, comic books, calendars--even if you intend to sell by way of your website, you'll need a business license. If you intend to pursue commercial work, especially at the local level, the client may need a copy of your license in order to meet his own tax filing requirements.

### Business Cards, Mailers, Portfolios, Product Catalogs

A Business Card has a single purpose: to archive contact information in a convenient and easily retrievable manner. Potential clients won't generally take the time to find a magnifying glass so they can read the phone number printed in tiny, little letters and folded beneath a reproduction of a painting that probably lost most of its definition in the reduced printed size.

Your business card had better introduce you as a professional or it'll wind up unread and pitched into that small metal can we all generally keep in the corner. Don't scrimp on the cardstock. People are likely to immediately dispose of a card that isn't pleasant to the touch. You don't have to print on the most expensive stock you can find, but pick something substantial enough to suggest you're a success.

Another effective introductory tool is the mailer. This is the package you'll send to galleries seeking representation, to art directors seeking free-lance work and to retailers seeking to place your product--greeting cards, etcetera--into their place of business. Or it could be simply a reminder card that you're available, or an invitation to visit your website to preview your newest work. One more time: if you aren't on the premises, your printed material doesn't represent you, it is you. Faded colors printed on cheap newsprint not only fail to present your work to best advantage, they suggest the package came via way of an amateur.

Assemble your promotional material with the most impressive material you can reasonably afford. It better to have a well-produced two-page mailer than a shoddily produced six-pager.

And make sure your contact information is easily found and easily read.

Computer technology and the internet has drastically changed the manner in which the artist presents his portfolio to a prospect. Yes, if you're meeting face-to-face you'll want to bring a professional portfolio with original work, but chances are you'll conduct more business these days by phone, website and email than in person.

If you're using an online portfolio to showcase your work, remember that exposing your artwork is the site's primary purpose. You're selling either your art skills or the results of those art skills, not trying to impress a gallery director or an art director with your web building abilities. Simpler is better. And if you're selling product from your website, separate your portfolio from your selling pages so the Gallery Director or the Art Director doesn't have to wade through a sales pitch for private label t-shirts and lunchboxes.

It's often a good idea to provide samples--sort of a mini-portfolio--that the prospect, especially the art director, can file and retrieve for future use. One more time: good materials, good color reproduction and easily accessed contact information. An effective sample catalog can be assembled the same way you would assemble a product catalog, but without pricing information.

## Copyright, Trade Mark & Work for Hire

A copyright protects an original artistic or literary work.

Copyright is a form of protection provided by the laws of the United States to the authors or creators of original works, including literary, dramatic, musical, artistic, and certain other intellectual works. A completed work is automatically copyrighted, but that copyright must be registered to insure ownership and legal protection. This protection is available to both published and unpublished works. The Copyright Act gives the owner of the copyright the exclusive right to do and to authorize others to do the following:

- To reproduce the work
- To prepare derivative works based upon the work
- To distribute copies of the work to the public by sale or transfer of ownership, or by rental, lease, or lending
- To display the copyrighted work publicly

It is illegal for anyone to violate any of the rights provided by the copyright law to the owner of copyright, meaning that copyrighted material cannot be used without the permission of the copyright owner. There are, however, limitations on these rights. In some cases, these limitations are specified exemptions from copyright liability. One major limitation is the doctrine of "fair use". In other instances, the limitation takes the form of a "compulsory license" under which certain limited uses of copyrighted works are permitted upon payment of specified royalties and compliance with statutory conditions. Copyright issues can become increasingly complicated and this manual isn't designed to be a legal referendum on the issue. For further information about the limitations of any of these rights, consult the copyright law or write to the Copyright Office. A bulk of information--and the downloadable forms to file for copyright filing--is accessible at http://www.copyright.gov/ .

Artwork and photographs are usually copyrighted using Form VA. It is permissible to copyright more than one image per form. Each filed form necessitates a filing fee, so copyrighting multiple images on the same form can result in an immediate savings. Remember, the less you spend the more you make. The work would be copyrighted as a compilation using the title, for example, *Douglas Ready's Studio Work, September 2011.*

Copyrighted work should be marked with the proper copyright notice. The notice consists of three parts: (1) either the symbol © (preferred because it also suites the requirements of the Universal Copyright Convention), the word Copyright or the abbreviation Copr.;(2) the year of first publication; and (3) the name of the copyright owner. Stated simply, a proper copyright notice looks like this:

*©Douglas Ready 2011*

Copyrighted work should always be displayed with the proper copyright notice. Reproductions of the original image should always note the registered copyright. The copyright notice informs the viewer that all rights pertaining to use and reproduction of the image are retained by and reserved to the copyright owner. If there is no visible copyright notice, the viewer may well assume the image is in the Public Domain, i.e., for all intents and purposes belongs to no one in particular and its use is fair game. A lack of a posted copyright notice is generally a viable defense for copyright infringement.

A trademark is a word, phrase, symbol or design, or a combination of words, phrases that identifies and distinguishes the source of the goods or products of one party from those of others. A service mark is the same as a trademark, except that it identifies and distinguishes the source of a service rather than a product.

You can establish rights in a mark based on legitimate use of the mark. However, owning a federal trademark registration on the Principal Register provides several advantages, e.g., constructive notice to the public of the registrant's claim of ownership of the mark; a legal presumption of the registrant's ownership of the mark and the registrant's exclusive right to use the mark nationwide on or in connection with the goods and/or services listed in the registration; the ability to bring an action concerning the mark in federal court; the use of the U.S registration as a basis to obtain registration in foreign countries; and the ability to file the U.S. registration with the U.S. Customs Service to prevent importation of infringing foreign goods.

Any time you claim rights in a mark, you may use the "TM" (trademark) or "SM" (service mark) designation to alert the public to your claim, regardless of whether you have filed an application with the United States Patent and Trademark Office (a patent protects an invention).  However, you may use the federal registration symbol "®" only after the USPTO actually registers a mark, and not while an application is pending.  You can file your application directly over the Internet using the Trademark Electronic Application System (TEAS) available at http://www.uspto.gov/teas/index.html .

A work for hire describes a situation where the artist is retained to create a specific piece of work that will upon completion be owned in its entirety by another party.  The artist's compensation is dependent upon transfer of ownership and all rights to the artwork to that party--in other words the artist is paid a one time fee and waives any future claim to the work, including any say in the use of the imagery on subsidiary products, and residuals or commissions on that subsidiary usage. The party that retained the artist owns the image lock, stock and barrel and can do with it as they darn well please.

**Agents, Attorneys & Other Professional Hazards**

Let me get this in right up front:  Art Agents don't do anything for the artist the artist cannot do for himself, and probably more effectively.  Most agents will tell you differently.

The simple truth is that the baton for directing your career is probably best left in your own hands.  I'm quite certain there's an agent out there who's worth every penny of the 20-25% you'll wind up paying him--plus expenses, in most cases--

but in twenty-plus years in the art business, I've yet to meet him.

It isn't that art agents are inherently evil, it's just that they aren't necessary. There are instances when an art agent's negotiating skills could work to the artist's advantage, but negotiation skills--like sales and marketing--is an attribute reasonably easy to acquire. Dropping your career development strategy into anyone's hands other than your own can be a recipe for disaster. Any agent generating enough commission to earn a living from his efforts must by necessity represent a stable of artists, thus defusing his efforts to enhance a single career. The artist who refuses to accept responsibility for building his own career often discovers that he has become just another notch on an agent's list and is missing out on important opportunities simply because he himself isn't chasing them.

And forget about signing with an agent and chasing appropriate work yourself. The industry standard is for the agent to require his full commission on any project the artist tackles while signed, regardless of its source.

In the greatest majority of cases, art directors are directly approachable. The artist willing to assume responsibility for marketing his own abilities and negotiating his own pay rates will usually have a more secure and successful career than the artist who shoves that responsibility in another direction, crosses his fingers and hopes for the best.

That said, there is one area where an agent can significantly increase the probability of success: book publishing. If your ambitions include writing and illustrating children's books--assuming you're looking to create your project from scratch, not just to secure an illustration assignment from a publisher--or humor books or even how-to art books, an agent is often a necessity for securing the best working contract.

Please note the difference between the Literary Agent and the Art Agent. If you're trying to sell a book, you don't want the presentation and the negotiations handled by someone whose primary experience is hawking your drawing ability to an ad agency.

Access to an attorney with experience in intellectual property, specifically art and design, is paramount. Attorneys specialize in different areas of law, and even in different areas of contract law. Think of it in medical terms: you wouldn't trust a Proctologist to surgically remove your tonsils, and you don't want to trust an attorney without experience dealing with those areas that will directly affect your career and your income. Take the steps now to identify several attorneys with appropriate experience before you need to speak with one of them--that way, you know who to call. In a crisis situation, you're more likely to settle for an attorney who just isn't qualified to properly deal with your concerns.

Eventually, once you begin to achieve some measure of success in selling your artistic endeavors, you'll find yourself confronted by any number of promoters, referrers, coordinators-- in short, people who neither purchase art outright nor offer assignments--who will assure you they can enhance your visibility by introducing you to any number of potential clients. You'll also find that any number of art agents who wouldn't consider adding you to their roster prior to your self-won published accomplishment are now miraculously enchanted by your work and are certain they can manage your career a good deal more effectively than you've managed to do on your own.

If you're bound and determined to hand the reins of your career over to someone else, at least use some common sense. Any agent asking for more the fifteen percent (15%) of the work he or she specifically generates for you should probably be sidestepped.

Licensing Agents generally want fifty percent (!) of whatever licensing deal they drum up. Brings to mind P.T. Barnum's most often quoted remark...

Get everything in writing--dollar amounts, percentages,

payment schedules, copyright ownership, and--just as important--specific terms for terminating the relationship.

And one more rule of thumb: anybody who asks for money to promote you should be dismissed.

**Festivals, Street Fairs, Trade Shows & Conventions**

There are any number of Trade Shows held annually. The focus varies depending on the group involved. The art publishing industry, the book publishing industry, the advertising industry, the magazine publishing industry, the newspaper publishing industry--all have their own Trade Shows, as does the Stationery industry, the movie industry, the fashion industry and just about any other industry you can think of.

Trade Shows can be a good venue for meeting potential clients, but participation is not generally inexpensive and the geographical location of the shows can be prohibitive. Trade journals for each industry regularly report on Trade Shows and the artist with a bent toward exploring this promotional vehicle would do well to study the journals with a jaundiced eye and determine whether or not the cost of attending warrants the potential return.

Conventions, on the other hand, are ready-made for the artist who specialized in genre work. I'm not talking about the meeting the sales guys go to without their wives, I'm talking about the literally thousands of conventions held every year as an opportunity to gather the fan base of any number of genres--comic book readers, civil war aficionados, science fiction and fantasy buffs, historical societies, renaissance people--this is where they gather in kind and in bulk.

These events offer the artist an opportunity to present--and offer for sale--that work designed for a specific audience in a venue that pretty much guarantees every pair of eyes in the hall will be interested in his subject matter. That doesn't necessarily mean that every pair of eyes will be interested in the artist's particular style, but in this kind of concentrated fan base the odds of stumbling across someone who does like your style improve greatly.

## Source Books

The industry standard for the working artist to source potential clients is the Artists Market. This nominally priced annual volume is now available in several different varieties, including the Children's Writer & Illustrator's Market. These volumes are not necessarily complete within themselves, but they do offer contact information for a substantial number of the markets available to both the fine artist and the illustrator.

The Advertiser's Index is an invaluable source book for the illustrator interested in advertising or product design. This annual volume lists every company in the United States that spends a minimum of $50,000 a year on advertising. Contact information on each company usually includes the art director and the product development director, as well as information on which advertising agency handles that company's account. This book is expensive--better than $1000 a copy--but the business section of most public libraries will have a copy available.

Any number of industry trade journals publish an annual directory. Toys, Hobbies & Crafts, for example, publishes a toy industry directory that includes contact information on manufacturers, distributors--helpful for the entrepreneurial artist who has decided to use his design skills to produce and market a functional product--importers, specialty design firms and licensing firms--helpful if you've developed a character you'd like to license across the board for use on existing product. Specialized business information can be pricey, so it is recommended the artist check with the business section of his local library before purchasing these directories.

The publications necessary to build your career depend on the specific areas you intend to pursue. If posters and prints are a primary interest, Art Business News should be on your reading list. If comic books and graphic novels beckon to your creative abilities, The Comics Journal, Diamond Distributor's Previews and The Comic Buyers Guide should come in once a month. A quick Internet search on any specific discipline of artistic endeavor using the Google search engine (www.google.com) will direct the artist to any number of viable referral sources.

## Artists & Illustrators Directories

There are any number of creative directories--such as American Showcase or Creative Illustration-- in which the artist may purchase page space to showcase his work. Hopefully, these directories wind up in the hands of an art director looking to hire.

Other directories, such as Spectrum or The Best American Fantasy Illustration are released annually and sold to the general public in bookstores. These volumes can wind up on an art director's bookshelf, but are probably more useful in attracting potential retail customers to the artist's website.

The artist needs to carefully weigh the cost of inclusion in these directories before committing himself. These kinds of directories can prove helpful, but an effective, properly targeted direct marketing program can often produce the same kind of results at a more reasonable cost.

## Establish a Presence

Charisma is best defined as the ability to make others feel good about themselves. Charisma is a necessity for the artist whose work demands a public persona.

Art buyers want to know they're dealing with a successful creative person, and it's the artist's responsibility not to disappoint them. We enhance our ability to enchant the buying public when we create a personal and individual characterization that invites imaginary partnership.

The artist who is recognized as successful is one who understands the possibilities inherent in media exposure. A key to success in any business is the simple fact that people know who you are and what you do. Well, and probably where to find you if they have a need for what
you do.

Every community has a structured communication system, a network of newspapers, magazines, television and radio. The artist who learns to effectively utilize these tools will find the task of generating an income from his work a much easier task.

### Press Releases

A press release is a most effective and vital means of communication. In our modern world of multimedia, a newspaper still provides one of the best ways of sending a message out to the general public. You can get your exhibition and product release announcements published regularly if you write interesting, newsworthy press releases.

If you are just starting a relationship with a newspaper, you  need to call the newspaper to find out who to send a press release to, and what their deadlines are. You can send the release to a particular person, or you can simply send it to the Managing Editor.

Newspapers receive massive amounts of print material daily, and editors have to pick and choose what information is really of interest to their readers. An editor would much rather read a good press release than get a call and a request for a time-consuming meeting. Although it is always good to develop a rapport with your local press, you need to walk a fine line between making and maintaining a relationship with an editor, and making a pest of yourself.

Don't call an editor just to find out if your press release

arrived--assume it did. If you aren't getting enough press coverage, it probably means your press releases are weak, and you need to work on your writing skills.

A press release should be typed or word processed on an 8 1/2": x 11 ": paper. Provide wide margins and double-space the copy. Use your business stationery--white paper, not some off-color stock that might prove difficult to read.

Use letterhead stationery or type the name, address, and telephone number of your organization, single-spaced, in the left margin of the page. This is the source of the press release. Also include the publicist's name and telephone number. This is the contact. If you do use a letterhead, but be sure to remember to include the contact's name and phone number.

If you need to promote something that is extremely time-sensitive, write specific details, such as:

### *RELEASE JANUARY 21*

It is also a good idea to suggest a headline. Although your headline might not be used, it immediately tells the editor, at a glance, what is the most important element of your press release.

The first sentence of your press release must be short and succinct, and get the message across in one fell swoop. Generally speaking, you'll use the first sentence to get the message out and one or two additional sentences to fill in the details. A press release is an announcement, not the Book of the Month.

Sometimes, your press release will require photographs. Be sure that every photo you send has a typed caption with appropriate identification information adhered to its back. Do not paper clip or staple the photo to the press release, just toss the photo into the envelope with the press release.

Editors are inundated with press releases. It's a good

idea to send a thank-you letter to the editor who places your press releases in the paper. After all, the day will come when you'll want the editor to place your next press release.

Most local television and radio stations have some kind of broadcast segment that allows the announcement of items of interest. Present your announcement to these venues and locally published magazines in the same manner you'd approach the newspaper editor.

More importantly, most every television station broadcasts a local talk show. An appearance on local programming lends an air of celebrity to the artist, an unquestionable asset to the artist with a new exhibition or a new poster release.

A quick call to your local television station will identify the proper party to send your press release to. State simply that you'd like to appear on the program and list several reasons why you think the audience would have an interest in your appearance. If the producers are interested, you'll usually receive a telephone call--in actuality a screening interview. With a little luck, you'll be invited to the station for an exploratory interview to determine your suitability for inclusion as a program guest.

Most local cable television concerns host a Public Access broadcast channel. Public Access is a system mandated by the Federal Communications Commission to help assure media access to those who might normally be denied such access. The cable company is required to provide facilities and training to those interested in producing their own television show. If your personality is such that hosting a self-produced weekly half-hour television program might be an enjoyable pursuit, the promotional opportunities should be obvious.

**The Website**

The Internet has greatly expanded the potential for

entrepreneurial success, particularly for those businesses that are singularly driven.  A primary vehicle for pursuing this success is the web site and the key to achievement in this arena is exposing the web site to as many appropriate viewers, i.e., potential customers as possible.

The website's sole function is to effectively showcase the artist's work.

Regardless of the design specifications and functional anomalies, the web site must load quickly, capture the viewer's attention within just a few seconds, be easy to maneuver through and readily demonstrate the desirability of the artwork displayed.  Aesthetics are important to creative people and sometimes there is a tendency to focus more on the creation of the web site than its function.  Whirling bits of animation, complicated mazes of boxes designed to lead the viewer from one gallery to another or pop-up boxes designed to regale the viewer with whatever visual wizardry conceived by the web designer who took your money are virtually guaranteed to drive away the potential shopper and prevent his or her return.

There are two methods of web site promotion: Direct and Indirect.

Direct Promotion refers to making the best use of those established procedures designed to help the seeker readily identify and locate those sites appropriate for his needs, i.e., Search Engines and Referral Sites.

The most effective tool in the Direct Promotion of a website is the Search Engine.  Search Engines gather information on existing web sites by either scanning a list of keywords supplied by the Web Master at the time of registration or by scanning the words on the first page of the web site itself. It is, therefore, of utmost importance to post copy on the first page of your site that states in no uncertain terms who you are and what you do.

Registering your site with a Search Engine is a relatively

quick process. Simply go the main page of the Search Engine and look for the icon that says something to the effect of "Register a Site". Click on the icon and follow the instructions. Some Search Engines will offer a "Priority" for a fee, either quicker consideration of your site for inclusion or sometimes a promise to list your site sooner when a query is posted rather than later in the list. You'll have to make your own determination as to whether or not you wish to spend the money, but just registering your site without a financial investment is usually appropriate. If you find yourself registering with a Search Engine that demands a registration fee, back out immediately.

There are literally dozens of Search Engines. Many of them pool resources so registering your site with one automatically registers it with several others. It is recommended that the greeting card entrepreneur take the time to register--in no particular order--with Google, Yahoo, Ask.com, AOL Search, and WebCrawler. These particular Search Engines seem to be the favorites among those looking on the internet. Furthermore, it is recommended that the site be re-registered with each of those Search Engines every 90 days. There is some evidence that the more recently a site has been added, the more likely that site is to appear early in Search Engine queries.

If you're selling product from your website, organize the site into two sections: a portfolio section and a catalog section. Visitors who are considering contracting you for commercial services aren't generally interested in wading through the thirty poster images you're pushing. In fact, the notion that you've referred an art director to a selling catalog is could be enough to give him second thoughts about contacting you for future work.

If you're going to sell from your site, make it easy for your customers to buy. If the only payment method you're setting up is to print out and order form and mail a check, you're going to lose a lot of potential customers. If product variety warrants, set up an online shopping cart, but at the very least insert a PayPal icon for each item. PayPal also allows buyers to make purchases from your site using Credit Cards.

If you are selling product directly to consumers on the site, consumers should be directed to their own section. If you're selling wholesale on the site, it's a good idea to have a separate wholesale section. Post a link on the first page of your site that will take the wholesaler to where he needs to be, just as you posted a link that will carry the art director to a simple portfolio section.

A printable order forms is a must, even if you're set up for online ordering. Give your customers the option of ordering in whatever manner is comfortable for them.

Clearly state minimum order requirements. Tell your customers approximately how long they'll have to wait for merchandise, retail or wholesale, and make certain the orders go out in a timely fashion.

If you're interested in talking with distributing firms, convey that information on a separate and distinct page from the other pages.

Imagine yourself standing inside a retail store at a greeting card display. If inflated promotional objects popped out at you every time you attempted to remove a card from the rack for consideration or if the rack began to spin every time you reached for a card, you'd probably leave.

So will most web surfers.

The idea is to make it as easy as possible for the potential customer to peruse your samples. Remember, he isn't there because he's looking to be impressed with your marvelous ability to create a website. Don't let the web site become so annoying that actually looking at your artwork is the last thing a visitor would consider.

It's been estimated that you've got eight seconds to capture a web surfer's attention--if you're lucky. Every loading delay you build into your site increases the possibility that he'll be gone before the entire site is visible. Don't assume most visitors have high-speed internet access. In fact, it's a good idea to log into one of the sites that offers no-cost limited internet access--like NetZero--sign up and connect to the internet using their dial-up system. This is an easy way to find out just how long potential customers might be waiting to get a look at your product.

*SPAM* is an annoying fact of life. Most of us utilize some sort of screening software to sort out those unwanted solicitations and they are deleted without being read. It's perfectly legal to send a one-time email invitation to visit your web site to a party you don't know, but unless you can do it in multiples of hundreds of thousands your return on the effort is bound to be negligible. You'll realize a much better return by offering an emailing list on your site so visitors who already have an interest in what you have to offer know when to return to take a look at your updated products.

Print advertising has proven extraordinarily ineffective as a means of securing visitors to your website. The simple truth is that people who chance upon your site while they are online are much more likely to visit than people who find your URL in a magazine and have to write it down and remember to punch in the web address the next time they venture online.

Indirect Promotion refers to making the best use of secondary functions to help the seeker identify and locate those sites appropriate for his needs. Your greeting cards or posters are products and their primary function is to be sold, but an effective secondary function is as a promotional beacon, a beacon lit by the placement of your web address on the back of each individual card or listed in small type at the bottom of your poster. Someone who has already purchased a reproduction of your art is likely to consider a future purchase and a quick referral to your online catalog is a good way to make that next purchase an easy thing to do.

There are online chat groups focused on most any subject or endeavor. A quick perusal of the Yahoo Group Page will identify sometimes hundreds of groups of like-minded folks who may have an interest in your product. You make photo cards with horses on them? Common sense suggests that an Equestrian Chat Group might have a few members who'd be interested in buying from you. Or a Rodeo Group. Or a group of Horse Racing Enthusiasts. There is generally no charge for joining any of these online chat groups and membership may prove beneficial to you in other areas as well. SPAMMING the members of a chat group isn't appropriate, but an introductory notice on the Message Board with a subdued invitation to visit your website for a look at what you do certainly is. Chat Groups, sometimes called Message Boards, are sponsored by a number of different online operations and easily identified using the Group Search function of the Search Engine Google.

A number of online operations, such as Yahoo and Hotmail, provide free email services, and this service is often accompanied by the offer of a free web page. There are also online companies--Lycos Tripod comes to mind--determined to offer you a free web page in the hopes that you'll eventually use them as your primary web site carrier. Generally, selling product from these pages is prohibited, but posting a couple of your more popular images on the free web page and posting a link to your main web site, giving the web surfer the opportunity to peruse more of your work, is certainly acceptable. Remember, every free web page you construct has the potential of directing new customers to your main web site, and these are to be set up strictly as referral sites--a one-time setup with no maintenance involved. In fact, you'll probably never visit that web page again once you've set it up.

A variety of online companies seek to partner with creators. Companies like Cafe Press offer the opportunity to place your designs on products they produce and sell for a commission through their own web site. While a real opportunity for profit to the creator might be dubious, most of these companies offer a free web page to showcase your image on their products and will allow you to post a link to your web site on that page.

On occasion, you'll receive a request to use one or more of your images on someone else's website. These kinds of requests generally come from non-commercial sites from someone who became enchanted with your work. Consider allowing the use of your work in exchange for credit and a link back to your web site listed with the image.

Take advantage of every no-cost online opportunity to post a referral to your web site.

Finally, a few observations that should prove useful:

Every effort should be made to make your visitors want to revisit your site. Change the content every 30 days or so, even if all you do is to move everything around for a different aesthetic. Your visitor won't remember everything that was on the site anyway, but he will generally notice if it doesn't look like the site has been changed.

Get that Visitor Counter off of your site! A new visitor who finds out he's the thirty-fourth one to hit your site may figure there must be nothing there worthwhile or you'd be getting more traffic. Believe me, he won't wait for the rest of the page to load. An invisible counter you can access from behind the site will tell you how much traffic you're getting. Anyway, those numbers are nobody's business but your own.

Establish a Visitor's Log and offer a signup block for an Email List. People who sign your log do so because your product appeals to them. Most people won't take the time to sign up if they don't think they might have a future need for your product. In fact, people who'll voluntarily signup for even more email deposited into their Inbox probably have a definite thought in mind for the future. Email a "Thank You" to everybody who signs the log or signs up for the mailing list--you can compose a standard response and have the message sent automatically.

Don't Make the Visitor's Log Available for Public Viewing. In the first place, some of your more ambitious competitors are perusing Visitor's Logs to determine who might be in the market for an introductory email invitation, and second, you don't want a visitor leaving your site having just read a nasty comment posted by some disgruntled fifteen-year-old kid.

Promoting yourself and your product on the Internet requires the same dedication and attention as promoting the physical product in the local market. The difference is that the Internet allows access to customers worldwide and the biggest promotional cost is time.

Your website is one of the most effective--and inexpensive--sales and marketing tools at your disposal. It gives you the opportunity to put your skills and the results of those skills in front of everyone in the world that has access to a computer, and all without print cost.

Your website should certainly contain every appropriate image you have available. Those images should be easy to access without a lot of splashy animation involved in the web page setup to aggravate those potential customers who find their way to your site. The concentration span of the modern consumer is extremely short--this isn't meant as an insult, but rather an observational statement of fact--and if your visitor has to wait longer than a few seconds for your page to load, chances are that he won't.

Your URL should be listed on every piece of business paraphernalia associated with your business: business cards, promotional pieces, catalog pages, invoices, packing slips, and definitely on your letterhead.

## Galleries and Other Myths

There is the thought among many artists determined to produce only work generated by their own internal mechanisms that to succeed in the art world gallery representation is a must. The truth is that only a very small percentage of working artists will ever acquire gallery representation. A much smaller percentage will acquire adequate gallery representation.

And, even if you're successful in finding that one gallery with which you can build a working relationship, the gallery won't do all the work. You need to check in regularly with the owner, build a rapport, meet potential buyers, attend openings, and reassure yourself that enough is being done to promote your work. In fact to insure success in a gallery environment you'll need to promote yourself at least as much as before you secured gallery representation.

The belief that you can pitch your art, without qualification or recommendation, to galleries until someone falls in love with it to the point where they take on your business affairs and leave you to toil happily away in the studio is a fantasy. Galleries are not in business to discover new and exciting creative geniuses and micromanage their respective careers. Galleries exist to sell art.

Galleries are only interested in art they believe they can sell, and there is only one known manner of proving your work will sell: somebody has to have bought some of it, preferably a good many pieces of it. An adequate gallery will work with the artist to build his client list, but very few of them are much interested in starting from scratch. Securing reputable gallery representation without an existing client list is virtually impossible.

I refer to reputable gallery representation. There are always so-called galleries willing to take on the work of any artist for a fee. The artist pays the gallery up front for wall space and promotional expenses, and is even expected to pick up the tab for the wine and cheese required on opening night. This variety of so-called gallery makes its money by cashing your check and actually does little more than sell you wall space, although most are perfectly willing to charge an additional commission--up to 50% in some instances--should a piece of your work sell. This kind of operation is sometimes referred to as a Vanity gallery.

The artist will do better with a Co-op gallery. This gallery is run and maintained by the artists who display on its walls. There is generally a fee to join, and the artist can expect to pay what amounts to monthly rent for the privilege of hanging his work on the wall. The artist may also be expected to man the gallery a few days every month. The Co-op will also charge a percentage of the dollars generated when and if the work sells, and while the percentage varies from Co-op to Co-op it is generally a smaller percentage than a traditional or Vanity gallery.

At any rate, whether the artist chooses to pursue traditional gallery representation or join a Co-op gallery the one thing needed to insure success is a client list, and the artist himself is the most effective tool available for generating a client list.

Identify an Audience

Most working artists earn a living without gallery representation. The practical artist learns very quickly that he and he alone is responsible for the success or failure of his artistic ventures and that while gallery representation is one way to put his work in front of collectors it certainly isn't the only way. Sometimes, it's not even the preferred way.

To be successful, the artist must secure collectors as clients. In order to secure clients, the artist must first identify an audience. An audience is a collection of people who are interested in or fascinated by or obsessed with the work the artist creates. A client is a member of that audience who actually took money out of his pocket and traded it to the artist in order to acquire a work of artistic creation.

You cannot and will not acquire clients until you've identified an audience.

### Identify an Audience

There is a market for every variety of art the artist can possibly create, but that doesn't necessarily mean there's an extensive market for every category of work. It is very possible to earn a substantial living producing a niche product, but the smaller the niche the more necessary it becomes for the artist to identify members of that niche if he is to prosper working only within that genre. If the artist is determined to produce nothing but highly detailed realistic scenes from the battle at the Alamo, he'd better identify every organization that studies or celebrates that particular brawl and make an effort to put samples of his work in front of every member of each organization, all the while keeping his fingers crossed. On the other hand, if the artist expands his repertoire to include not only the Alamo, but perhaps the Civil War his potential audience amplifies to the point of potential viability.

The successful artist will take the necessary steps to discern and pursue that portion of the populace with a potential interest in his product.

### Originals, Prints and Posters

If the artist is determined to sell directly to collectors those images created from his own internal directives, there are three varieties of product available for promotion: originals, prints and posters.

Selling the original art is a straightforward undertaking. The artist creates the work and exchanges it with a buyer for a mutually determined price.

A valuable addendum is the print. Prints may be hand-pulled or commercially printed, and are produced in a limited number, that number to be determined by the artist. The prints are signed and numbered on the front of the print to indicate both the number of the print and the number of prints created, i.e.:

**24/75**

*(indicating print number 24 out of an edition of 75 prints)*

Prints are sold at a less expensive price point than the original work, making the print a more affordable, and sometimes a more appealing alternative to acquiring the original artwork. Prints, like the original art, have the potential to increase in value as the artist becomes more established.

Posters differ from prints in the fact that they are not limited to a particular number of copies. Generally, posters are reproduced on a less costly grade of paper than prints, but not always. Posters are an inexpensive way to make your work accessible to large numbers of people who for whatever reason aren't interested in spending the necessary amount of money to acquire an original piece of artwork.

Thanks to modern printing technology, the only real difference between a print and a poster is often the signature and the numbering. There is an ongoing discussion regarding the proper categorization of commercially reproduced limited edition work. Some feel that only the print hand-pulled by the artist should be referred to as a print, that the commercial reproduction, regardless of its quality, is nothing more than a signed and numbered poster. The distinction is one the artist will have to determine for himself.

**Reproduction Rights**

The artist has a much better chance of generating a reasonable income if he remains open--in fact actively pursues--reproduction opportunities for his work. Prints, posters, greeting cards, collectors' plates--all reproduction possibilities, and that income potential, are dependent upon the artist retaining reproduction rights to his work.

This means that someone who buys your original art that person must be informed that while the collector owns the artwork, the artist solely owns the right to reproduce the work and only the artist can sanction such reproduction. A simple written statement included in the Bill of Sale should be sufficient to accomplish this most important communication.

It is paramount for the artist to retain a copy of the artwork. In the event that reproduction rights are assigned, the artist will be expected to provide a viable image for the client to work with and it is unrealistic to expect the collector to return his property for the artist's use. Retaining a copy of the image is best accomplished by archiving computer scans that can be manipulated for future use as the occasion arises.

**Targeted Promotion**

Selling art is a difficult skill to master, but if you're going to make a living as an artist you have to be able to sell your art at least as well as you're able to create it.

I am astounded at the number of talented artists who have mastered their craft and produce absolutely wonderful creations, but know so little about how the art business works and what they have to do to sell their work that most of their working days are spent engaged in occupations that have absolutely nothing to do with the art world.

Students attend art school so they might learn to create art that is good enough to sell, believing that if a quality art education is pursued and acquired one can make a living as an artist. Art school offers a wonderful opportunity to spend several years practicing one's decided craft, but selling and marketing are seldom found in any art school curriculum.   Art school does not teach you how to how to sell your art in the real world. You'll probably learn how to put together a portfolio, but the chances of an instructor taking you aside and explaining just how to find the person who wants to purchase what's inside that portfolio are almost non-existent.

The student is told that if the work is good enough showing it to a gallery owner or mailing a reproduction to an art director is all that is necessary to generate income.   Some art schools dismiss the art business altogether by suggesting that creating art is where the artist's focus should be, that making money isn't pertinent to the process and debases the experience of being an artist. Schools rarely seem to mention that if you can't make money making art, you have to spend a good portion of your time engaged in unrelated dollar-generating activities.

Selling art does not diminish your credibility as an artist, it enhances it.

In the beginning, your day-to-day accomplishments are what advance your art career. Create to the best of your ability and get your work out there.   Display your artwork at every opportunity, hang it in every restaurant and bar that will let you use their wall space, set up at every street fair and art festival you can get to.  Listen to what people say, get a sense of who likes what and why, figure out how to price it so it sells, and show it whenever and wherever you get the chance. Along the way, you'll meet people, make connections, and those you impress the most will eventually introduce you to others who can do more for you.

That's how any business works, and the art business is no different.

There are as many ways to sell art and become successful as an artist as there are artists, and each and every one of those ways is perfectly acceptable.   The key to success is identifying those methods you can comfortably apply to your own work.

Most artists want to become rich and famous as soon as possible. They want to create art full time, basking in the solitude of their studios while other people sell it. In pursuit of this lofty goal, the number one question artists ask is how to get representation.  Most are stunned to discover that you have to sell art in order to attract gallery attention.  Once you learn to make sales--once you've learned to persuade others that your art has merit-- you'll be ready for representation.

You must learn to convince others that they're better off owning than not owning your art.  It is certainly gratifying to hear someone say they love your work, but compliments, no matter how constant, won't keep you from the need to pursue that career in food service.

The overwhelming majority of art world relationships are initiated through networking between people who already know each other. This is pretty much the same in any business. Few people are willing to take chances on total strangers and this is why cold calling rarely works unless you've developed a zealous sales personality or you have something unbelievably astonishing to cold call about.

All artists want to sell themselves and their art, but you'll have better luck selling when you sense that whomever you're speaking with wants to be sold to. You don't want to get a reputation for turning every conversation into a selling situation. People will see you coming and walk the other way or at least stop taking your telephone calls.

Art galleries sell art for a living.  They carefully evaluate every artist who presents them with art and decide to work only with those who can demonstrate that their art is not only salable, but that it will sell.

Art business professionals sell their art by convincing people that it has value and that it's worth paying money for in order to own. Rarely in the art business do people spontaneously buy art because they fall in love with it the moment they see it. They ask questions and whoever answers those questions has to answer them in ways that sell the art.

Art simply doesn't sell itself. Someone has to sell it.

The same holds true for you as an artist. Your art does not sell itself: you have to sell it. Selling your art involves much more than inviting someone to your studio or your website or setting up at a street fair or showing a gallery owner a portfolio of your work. When people see your art and like it, they automatically think about whether they can make money selling it, and you have to address that concern.

If you want a gallery to represent you, you have to convince that gallery that money can be made selling your art and that you can help them make that money. Your involvement in the process is essential. You have to address the financial implications of what happens to your art once it leaves your studio and goes to market. If you sit there grinning hoping you'll be offered a contract, you'll probably be sorely disappointed. You have to prove that you're a marketable commodity.

Proving your marketability is essential, but especially so if the person seeing your art has no idea who you are. To begin with, most artists get shows or representation by word of mouth. They're introduced to the people who eventually sell their art. If at all possible, get a personal introduction to gallery owner who you think should see your art.

With or without introductions, target only those galleries who sell your type of art or represent artists with comparable resumes and career accomplishments to yours. Know enough about the art they sell so that you can customize your presentation and explain why you believe your art is right for them. Be ready to explain why you picked a particular gallery to pursue representation and understand that flattery--because this gallery is the best there is--is not your strongest collaborator.

Personalize your presentation or chances are good that your presentation will go nowhere.

Talk about why you believe people will want to own your art. This doesn't mean that you do a high-pressure sales pitch, but rather that you treat the meeting as though you're looking to enter into a moneymaking partnership. If the only reason you've got for showing your art is that the person you're showing it to sells it, you're better off not making the presentation until you've rethought your position.

Describe the market for your art as well as you can. Talk about who buys it, why they like it, how much you sell, and how much it sells for. The more such information you provide, the better a prospective dealer, agent, gallery, or representative is able to evaluate whether they can sell your work.

### The Care & Feeding of the Collector

Most people won't spend a lot of money on something just because they like it. If Mr. and Mrs. Collector just want something in pale green to match the drapes there are much less expensive options open to them than purchasing an original piece of artwork. As an artist, you know what your art means on a personal level and you can certainly convey that to people, but are you able to justify your selling price? Explaining why your art has value from a monetary standpoint is an essential part of convincing buyers that your art is something they want to own, especially when they're undecided or unfamiliar with your work.

Many buyers, especially those perusing your work for the first time, need assurances because they often don't know that much about art. They're insecure and they want concrete facts presented in a manner they can understand. Some collectors, of course, buy art on the spur of the moment and according to whatever strikes their fancy, but they're in the minority. Be prepared to demonstrate that your art has value.

Documentation is a good first step. Do everything

possible to get your work reviewed. A feature in a newspaper or magazines, even a one-word mention in a small article at the bottom of the page in the local neighborhood newspaper helps establish your credibility.

Along with documenting your career accomplishments, document every significant piece of your art. Explain what the art is, what it's made out of, why you created it, what inspired you, what it represents. A couple of paragraphs accompanied by a photograph or two of the work in progress should do it. Include these with the art when you sell it. Collectors appreciate a little something extra and this provides them with a little something special, something personal that helps them understand they've just purchased a valuable piece of original art, not simply a wall decoration.

Keep track of individual works of art. Record who and when they sold, how much they sold for, any unusual circumstances regarding the sale. These records will come in extremely handy for your future promotional efforts.

Selling art is a competitive venture. If a collector has only $1000 to spend and he intends to buy only one piece of art, he's either going to buy it from you or he's going to buy it from another artist. Success depends on stacking the odds in your favor by increasing the chances that he's going to buy it from you.

Often this involves little more than being able to comfortably talk about your art. Most contemporary art collectors regard the experience and adventure of meeting and speaking with artists as an essential part of collecting. Collectors love getting involved in the art community by spending time at galleries, going to openings, visiting artists at their studios, crawling through street fairs, talking about art and meeting artists. With luck, the collector will feel something akin to a sponsor and begin presenting you to fellow collectors.

If you're uneasy in public situations or have problems

speaking about your art, practice with friends or associates. This is called Role Playing and although it's bound to feel silly while you're doing it, it's the best way to become comfortable with a process that's paramount to achieving success. Actors rehearse for a reason and that reason isn't just to memorize their lines.

The instant you complete a work of art and place it up for sale, it becomes subject to the laws of the marketplace just like any other goods or services. The artist must transition from the creative mode to the objective pricing mode. People like to know that they're getting good value for their money. This means that you've got to price your art competitively. A good rule of thumb, whenever you're not sure how much your art is worth, is to price comparably to what other artists with similar accomplishments and similar market bases to yours charge for similar works of art.

If you can't figure out how to price your art, pay yourself a sensible hourly wage, multiply that amount by the number of hours you take to make the art, toss in the cost of materials, and let that total be your asking price. Whatever formula you choose for pricing will undoubtedly require adjusting once you've had the opportunity to present your work to the buying public. Just don't make the mistake of pricing yourself out of the market before you get started. And, don't price your work so that people won't take you seriously.

You may want to experiment with different pricing structures. This gives you a chance to get outside feedback from collectors and settle on dollar amounts that make both you and your collectors feel the most comfortable. It's best to settle on a pricing structure as soon as reasonably possible, though, because the last thing you want is the collector who bought a piece at your last exhibition finding that a similar piece is 20% less expensive this time around.

**Courting the Gallery**

Many artists imagine that once they've acquired gallery representation all their problems will be solved. A team of professionals will devote themselves to selling the work and the artist can retire to the studio and devote himself solely to the creation of yet another masterpiece.

Dream on.

A gallery contract may require exclusive rights to sell your work, thus limiting your market. If you hold an open studio, you will be expected to sell at gallery prices, otherwise gallery clients may feel they are being overcharged for your work--and, the gallery may expect a commission from those sales. If you want to participate in a local exhibition, you will need to get the gallery's permission. And, you'll probably need their permission to seek gallery representation in other locals or to publish reproductions of your art.

You acquired gallery representation on the basis of a certain type of work and you'll be expected to continue producing in that style. You will also be expected to produce a certain amount of salable work, which can lead to undue pressure if you're subject to creative blocks.

That said, gallery representation can be an effective method of putting your work in front of people whose sole purpose for visiting the gallery is to purchase art.

Target the galleries you want to approach and remember that the process isn't one of convincing the gallery owner to look at your work, but rather convincing him to represent your work.

An application package to a gallery should consist of 10-20 slides, each neatly labeled with titles, dimensions and medium, your name and the year you completed the piece. The gallery will want to know they're reviewing your current work. Make sure your application package focuses on a particular body of work. If you mainly paint nudes, don't toss in those two landscapes you've got no matter how well they turned out.

Include a suggested retail price list that includes the gallery's estimated 50% commission and indicate whether the work will be sold framed or unframed.

Include an up-to-date art resume and a short statement about your work, nothing pretentious, just something that details your artistic viewpoint and a little about your working process.

Compose a simple, straightforward cover letter stating in no uncertain terms that you're seeking gallery representation and would like to meet with the gallery coordinator to explore the possibility.   DO NOT address the cover letter to Gallery Coordinator--call the gallery and secure the name of the proper individual.  Enclose a self-addressed stamped envelope for the return of your materials.

Successful galleries may receive several hundred application packages every month.  Don't be surprised if it takes some months for them to get back to you.  Perversely, it will probably take longer to receive a response if they're interested.

The chances of securing gallery representation, especially if you've never had gallery representation, are slim. Expect rejection, shrug it off, and send out the next package. Most artists who do manage to secure gallery representation have first gone through dozens of rejections.

Eventually, with perseverance and a little luck, you'll get a positive response inviting you in to talk with the gallery coordinator.  Remember throughout your presentation that the main reason someone decides to represent your art is that they think they can sell enough to make enough to help them stay in business. Either they think they can sell that art now or they think that by working with you, they'll be able to sell it at some point in the future, most likely the near future. The only way to get and maintain gallery representation that lasts for more than one show is for them to sell enough to make their efforts worthwhile.

## A Promotional Gameplan

If you're serious about pursuing gallery representation, you have to put your work in front of gallery coordinators. Every time your application package is rejected, you're one gallery closer to finding the one that wants to hang your work on their walls.

Artists are continually told that application packages should only go to one gallery at a time. Given the odds of any one gallery having an interest--or even the need--to acquire another artist for their roster, this simply makes no sense. The artist should put his work in front of as many galleries as he can realistically juggle. If two galleries contact you simultaneously requesting an interview, talk with both of them. Just because a gallery has an interest doesn't necessarily mean they're going to offer you a representation contract. And, you may not be satisfied with the terms of a particular proffered contract.

The bottom line is that the possibility of two galleries contacting you at the same time is very slim.

A good rule of thumb is to have twelve application packages circulating to galleries at all times. When a package is returned to you, immediately turn it around and get it out to the next gallery on your list.

If you run through all the galleries in the city you're in, try another. When you run through those, try another city, then another state. In the meantime, realize that a successful art career is not dependent upon gallery representation. Explore other venues for displaying and selling your work--restaurants, bars, banks, libraries, bookstores, art festivals, street fairs, juried shows and a website.

Above all, keep producing the very best work you can.

## Have Portfolio, Will Travel

Surviving in the commercial art venue requires the ability to steadfastly set aside one's ego and understand that the work itself is of paramount importance. This is not always the case in the gallery world where the artist's persona is often a broadcasted facet of the finished product.

An art director rents the artist's skills, but he purchases a product. Often, in the art director's mind, he is utilizing the artist's skills to 'flesh-out' a concept of his own that he simply lacks the tactile ability to construct and most anyone with decent rendering ability should be able to successfully present the art director's concept . In truth, the art director selects an artist whose skills will not only mesh, but augment his own concepts. Most art directors develop a list of those individuals whose often silent input prompts the concept into something spectacular.

Stated simply, a commercial artist's job is to make the art director look good. Even in the case of those publishers who generally do not assign work and the art director's primary responsibility is acquired appropriate finished work for the company, the artist will quickly find that any attempt at circumventing the art director's sense of aesthetics--making him look bad--will inevitably terminate the artist's working relationship with a given publisher.

Generally speaking, artists prefer to work alone. One of the job's benefits is the fact we're sacrifice some of his hard-won solitude.

Deadlines become a way of life. The artist will discover that deadlines are seldom scheduled in such a manner as to allow the fullest development the artist can muster. That scheduling is often less than convenient, and the artist will find himself toiling at his drawing board at something different than traditional working hours. Speed becomes almost as important a skill as the artist's other artistic talents, and personal flexibility becomes more so.

The artist who would devote his time to conceiving and rendering his own creations with the intent of selling a finished product to a publisher will share many of the daily dilemmas faced by the artist who pursues work-for-hire assignments. Inevitably, there will be demands to rework concepts, incorporating the art director's sensibilities, and there will be deadlines and meetings and last minute changes.

Of course, before the artist is entitled to complain about the pitfalls of freelancing as a commercial artist, he or she must first get an assignment.

**Seducing the Art Director:  Targeted Promotion**

Identifying those art directors with whom you as an artist may hope to successfully cultivate a working relationship isn't particularly difficult, but it can be particularly tedious. The search is made even more difficult if the artist has yet to develop a distinct working style.

Personality is and will always be a factor in determining just whom an artist will work with.  Most of us prefer to spend our time associating with like-minded individuals we enjoy being around and art directors are no different.  I'm willing to bet you've got a favorite restaurant and a favorite waitress who works at that restaurant.  If you find yourself walking into the place for Sunday brunch, you probably look for that waitress and ask to be seated in her section.  It isn't that the other waitresses can't take your order and haul your omelet to the table without dropping it on the floor; it's just that--all things being equal--your personality and that waitress's personality somehow clicked.  You enjoy the way she approaches her job and you enjoy the fact that she does it well and in a timely manner.  So, you ask for her.

It isn't necessary for every art director you want to work with to become overwhelmed with an urge to be in the same room with you, but it is necessary that the art director recognize your abilities as proficient and you as a professional.

Art directors, by necessity, tend to remember an artist's style. The more unique the work style, the more he will be remembered. The artist who has yet to develop a distinct and memorable work style is more likely to vanish into the slush pile. Yes, the down side of a distinct style is that everyone won't like it, but it's better to stand out among those who do appreciate your style than to blend into a crowd among those who can take it or leave it.

Professionals target their promotional efforts. The art director responsible for acquiring new greeting card designs probably isn't much interested in your sixty-four page graphic novel. It certainly doesn't hurt to have evidence of the novel's creation in your portfolio, but if you haven't taken the time to develop specific samples pertinent to the interview opportunity-- in other words, you didn't draw up any greeting cards--chances are you're wasting your time and the art allowed to tuck ourselves into the studio, elect our own course of action, schedule our own daily activity and not have to sidestep that aggravating co-worker that just about everybody who has a job is obligated to tolerate. The artist who would pursue commercial work can expect to director's time.

There are any number of ways of assembling a portfolio and any number of sources that recommend particular methods of assemblage. Any of them are appropriate as long as your portfolio properly showcases appropriate work to your current prospect.

Identifying those art directors with whom the artist can develop a working relationship is a paramount responsibility. Eventually, you may reach the point where it is no longer necessary to pursue potential clients because potential clients are pursuing you, but until that day comes the artist must perpetually submit, submit, submit and submit again.

**Ad Agencies**

Advertising is one of the most lucrative markets for freelancers. There are literally thousands of ad agencies, design and marketing firms and all of them rely on freelancers.

Advertising agencies offer a variety of assignment possibilities, ranging from simple illustration to label and package design to complex storyboards. The advertiser's goal is to sell a product or service and the artist with a heightened sense of translating spoken communication into pictorial persuasion will have a distinct advantage in this arena.

Normally, you'll be paid by the project, but there are those occasions where an agency prefers you work onsite at their location in which case they'll probably pay you by the hour. There are some variations, but generally the agency considers work done-for-hire, meaning they own the copyright and the artist retains no rights.

A common practice is to ask for work to be done on speculation or "on spec". This is a circumstance where the agency takes your rendering of their idea and presents it to a client--or a potential client--in the hope that the client will want the agency to then produce a campaign using that idea. Sometimes the agency will offer a nominal fee for spec work, but sometimes you'll be asked to do the spec work for consideration of receiving an assignment to do the contracted work should the client sign on. It is imperative that you understand and agree to payment arrangements before accepting any agency assignment.

**Publishers**

The publishing industry offers a wide variety of possibilities to the commercial freelancer. Assignments are conceived and dispersed; new possibilities are presented and purchased. The artist will need a highly developed sense of storytelling as well as solid rendering ability.

### Books

A detailed, realistic painting style is often all that is required to secure assignment for creating book covers, although stylized work remains quite popular. It's best to approach these potential clients with work created especially to showcase your ability to translate story into a visual punch. Try creating a cover for several of your own favorite volumes--books an art director is surely familiar with.

### Children's Books

There are literally dozens of volumes available suggesting approaches to securing work in Children's Book publishing. Generally, the artist either writes and illustrates his own story, adapts an existing story or fairy tale that is in public domain, or illustrates a story written by another author.

Publishers select the artist who will be responsible for illustrations, not the author of the book, the exception being in that instance when the author is also the artist. A common misstep is the notion that an unpublished author must pair with an artist prior to submitting his manuscript.

A wide variety of art styles graces the children's shelf at the bookstore, everything from photographic realism to simplistic cartooning, but the artist must be able to render the same characters in a wide variety of poses and situations.

### Magazines

There are more magazines published today than in any other point in history. This may be the easiest market for the freelancer to break into, assuming that your work has a distinct style.

Study those magazines you think you might have an

interest in submitting to. Every magazine has its own character and the illustrations featured much not only hook the reader into spending time with the feature, but also fit into that magazine's persona.

Magazines have become highly specialized and much more demanding in their requirements for illustration and the more targeted the artist's presentation the better the likelihood of securing freelance work. You'll have much better luck approaching those magazines whose editorial tone is a good fit with your drawing style.

Generally speaking, the larger the circulation rates of the magazine the better the pay rate for freelance illustration. That said, the beginning freelancer may find that targeting trade magazines and regional publications is a more immediate lucrative pursuit. They pay reasonably well for work produced and the competition isn't as severe. Alternative weeklies, sometimes published in newspaper format, are good initial prospects as well. They don't pay as well, but working with an alternative publication will give you an opportunity to learn how to effectively communicate with art directors, develop a portfolio of published work in your distinct style and give you an opportunity to become accustomed to working on a deadline.

### Prints & Posters

Every picture framing store in the world either stocks prints and posters or has a series of catalogues tucked under the front counter for customers to peruse. Posters are increasingly popular for use in commercial venues thanks to the option of a less expense makeover accomplished by simply changing the posters hanging on the walls.

The public holds a broad appetite for content, so this publishing category offers possibilities to a wide variety of styles and subject matter, from the delicate watercolors of Steve Hanks to the whimsical fantasy of Real Musgrave and the bold strength of James Baldwin. If you're open to studying trends and actively working to produce commercial images this market can produce a healthy financial return quickly and consistently.

Most poster publishers are interested in reviewing series for consideration. If your painting of a rooster suddenly becomes the "flavor of the month" the publisher will want to quickly follow up with similar imagery produced by the same artist. And, smaller versions of a series are often framed and hung alongside one another in office hallways and restaurants.

The successful poster artist will need to study current trends to identify popular colors and themes.

### Greeting Cards & Notecards

It has been estimated that the Greeting and Note Card business generates some $5,000,000,000 in sales annually in the United States alone. That kind of volume eats up a lot or original art, everything from lighthearted cartoon designs to heartfelt renditions of family gatherings. Often, designs created for the Greeting and Note Card market translate well to other markets, specifically the Poster and Product Design markets.

Most every greeting card publishing company projects a distinct aura. Some focus on specifically holiday material, while others focus on religious ceremonies or simply the humorous aspects of everyday life. A big key here is simply making sure that the subject matter of your submission is appropriate to the company you're submitting to.

The industry standard size is 4 5/8" x 7 1/2" for artwork. It is permissible to submit in larger sizes, but the work needs to be scaled proportionately. Submissions in other than standard sizes will diminish the chance for a sale.

Some greeting card companies will request to purchase full rights to the work submitted. There is nothing inherently wrong with selling all rights as long as the artist is aware that the company then can produce other products--calendars or posters,

or they can even resell the rights for use by another company--
and the artist will have no recourse and generally no income
from that additional use.  If the artist is convinced that he can
sell the imagery for use on other product, signing away all rights
may not be the best way to go, depending on the dollars offered.
In either case, the artist needs to fully understand what rights
he's signing away.

### Coloring Books & Educational Workbooks

Coloring books generate a volume of work for a great
many artists.  The pay rates are often not kingly, but the art is
simple and straightforward and generally requires a fraction of
the time necessary to successfully complete other assignments.
The artist with an ability to subjugate own personal style to that
of stock or licensed characters will have a distinct advantage in
this market, and speed is essential, not so much because of
deadlines but because the pay rate per page is probably not
overwhelming.  It's necessary to produce a lot of pages to
generate a reasonable return.

There are of course those markets that produce generic
material.  The pay rate is generally even less, but these
companies produce a bulk of material and have an ongoing need
for freelancers.  If you have the ability to "whip out" simple line
drawings quickly, this is a good possibility for supplemental
income.

Educational workbooks--essentially coloring activity
books designed to be used with parental supervision in the
home--have become increasingly popular.  The illustrator is
usually provided a "script" and structures the book accordingly.

### Comic Books and Graphic Novels

The perception of Comic Books as a medium directed at
children has all but vanished.  Superheroes still dominate the
American market, but a plethora of material devoted to more

cogent subject matter can be found in most any bookstore. The comic book artist must be able to literally render everything, real or imagined. Whether producing material for so-called "long-john" characters or rendering humor material, comic book artists are among the most talented purveyors of the illustrators' art.

The major comic book companies farm work out in sections: one artist does the penciling, one does the inking, and another does the lettering. Coloring is done mostly with a computer these days.

The smaller companies generally seek a ready-made product, art and story and all the peripherals complete and ready for printing. They don't much care if the artist and the writer are the same person or not as long as they're presented with a viable story.

Storytelling is the hallmark of the comic book artist. Drawing ability is essential, but pictorial storytelling is what brings in the assignments, or in the case of an alternative work, what moves it off the shelves.

One estimate puts the number of comic books published every month in the United States at around 400 titles. Many of those books are what are referred to as Independent or Alternative books, which means that the book is published by other than the dozen or so major comic book publishers. Often, the creators of the book underwrite the cost of printing, promotion and distribution.

Graphic Novels are a more recent entry. Simplified, a graphic novel is a thick comic book. Comic books are traditionally 32 pages in length and are published on a regular publishing schedule, usually monthly or bi-monthly. A graphic novel is usually a minimum of 64 pages, may be printed on better quality slick paper--like a magazine--and may exist without a continuing publishing schedule, in fact may exist as what is referred to as a "one-shot", which means that the one book is what there is. There might be a follow-up, depending on how well the first volume sold, and there might not. Because of this, it's important that the story in a graphic novel is fully contained, that is begun and ended, within that issue.

The majority of comic books are sold through comic shops. At this writing, there is only one major distributor providing product to these retailers, Diamond Distributors, and if selling an alternative comic is your goal you'll need to follow Diamond's requirements very closely to convince them to carry your comic. The competition is overwhelming, but securing a recurring monthly assignment from a major publisher, DC or Marvel, to produce work for a popular book can catapult the artist into the upper strata of the income bracket for practicing illustrators. A popular alternative title can also be a vehicle for prosperity, but most of the money will generate from selling subsidiary rights--animation, action figures, and etcetera--than from sales of the comic book itself.

### Product Design

An arena often overlooked by artists is the area of product design. Everything from collectible plates and Christmas tree ornaments to dolls and stuffed animals are usually originated by a freelancer.

### Package Design

Package and label design is often handled by the company's Advertising Agency, but some companies handle these tasks in-house. The artist with a bent toward effective graphic and lettering design will have an advantage in this arena.

### Charities & Other Organizations

Organizations produce a bulk of printed material, whether that material is used for event promotion or fundraising. Charities generally do not pay kingly rates and are often overlooked by artists seeking assignment, but creating work for a charity is an excellent way to begin building a portfolio of published samples.

And, ongoing contributors are generally people with the means to purchase art for their own use. Working with a charity is an excellent method of extending your own personal following.

### Various & Sundry Unnamed Clients

Potential clients abound for the artist who will open his mind, his eyes and his ears.

Computer and Role Playing game makers need scads of artwork to illuminate new concepts and characters. Local garage bands need logos and flyers. Restaurants need menus redesigned. The local Medieval Society is sponsoring a three-day Renaissance Faire and needs an advertising poster--a bonus, in that the art can theoretically be used as a poster submission, greeting card art and possibly a t-shirt design.

Exact submission requirements and pay rates for any and all of these kinds of potential clients can be found in the current Artists' Market and online at specific company websites.

### Work for Hire

A work-for-hire describes a situation where the artist is retained to create a specific piece of work that will upon completion be owned in its entirety by another party. The artist's compensation is dependent upon transfer of ownership and all rights to the artwork to that party--in other words the artist is paid a one time fee and waives any future claim to the work, including any say in the use of the imagery on subsidiary products, and residuals or commissions on that subsidiary usage. The party that retained the artist owns the image lock, stock and barrel and can do with it as they darn well please. Most any commercial art assignment the artist is offered will be considered a work-for-hire.

That said, there are those instances when the artist creates an image solely of his own volition and decides to exploit that image for financial gain. Fabrics, party items such as paper plates, cups and napkins, a wide range of collectables, novelty items, t-shirts, wrist watches--all depend on eye-catching graphic enhancement, read ***pretty picture***, to help influence the consumer decision to purchase. Some greeting card designs are easily adapted as actual product designs for items such as toys, statuettes, puzzles, posters, and even fine art prints. Assigning reproduction rights for your imagery to companies involved in product manufacturing--as opposed to selling the company the design outright--is called *Licensing*.

## Licensing

Licensing allows you to fully exploit the imagery you've created, allowing more opportunity for additional income from that imagery without the need to launch an additional product line that you must manufacture and promote. You retain ownership of the image, but allow other companies to reproduce it on a particular product in exchange for monetary compensation. Think of licensing as renting your image for use on a specific product for a specified period of time. The company is responsible for manufacturing, promoting and selling the finished product.

Approaching a potential licensing client is much the same as approaching an Art Director to secure a free-lance assignment. The biggest difference is that in approaching a potential licensing client your objective is to sell him on using an image you've already produced as opposed to securing an assignment to produce work he might have in mind.

However, it isn't unusual to approach a potential licensing client who isn't interested in the imagery you're shopping, but appreciates your rendering style and asks if you'd be interested in doing free-lance work design for his company. In this instance, the company will generally consider all assignments a Work for Hire and will own the artwork and all rights from the moment you're compensated. The decision to accept work in this capacity as a free-lancer or not is a matter of personal choice.

The easiest way to identify potential licensing clients is to stroll through a retail store and take a look at what's on the shelf. If, for example, you think your designs would work well as puzzles, take a look at the puzzles you find in the stores and determine which puzzle manufacturers might use the kind of imagery you produce. Most every company has its specialty and puzzle manufacturers specializing in cartoon character puzzles for small children will usually have little interest in acquiring reproduction rights to a Fine Art quality photograph.

Licensing proposals are usually directed to either the Art Director or the New Product Development Director (exact titles vary, but they're close enough to jump out at you), and these folks are easily identified by checking the company listing in the *ADVERTISERS INDEX*, a volume that list contact information of every company in the United States that spends more than $50,000 annually in advertising. The book is expensive, but the Business Section of most libraries will have a copy. Or, telephone the company and ask to whose attention Licensing Proposals should be directed.

The proposal should contain a letter stating your intent and a copy of the imagery you're proposing for consideration. You'll want to enclose a copy of six different images per proposal package. Making several proposals while you've got a prospect's attention is just good business sense. It's sometimes a good idea to also enclose a reformatted version of an image, especially if you're proposing its use on a product with a specific shape, re, if you think your rectangular image would do well on a paper plate, it's probably a good idea to trim that image into a circle before submission. Reformatting helps make visualization for  the AD or the PDD a much simpler process.

Follow up the proposal package in the same manner you'd follow up any sample package you've mailed to an Art Director.  Enclose a self-addressed stamped envelope for the return of your samples in the event of non-interest.

So, let's assume you've connected with a company that's interested in using your art for their products.  They'll want you to read and sign a legal agreement that gives them the right to use your art--and perhaps even a bit more that you're not prepared for.  Licensing your imagery is a legal issue.  Many artists make mistakes that would have been completely avoidable if they had understood a few basic terms or if they had known how to read a licensing agreement. There are many holes that an artist can step into on the way to commercial success.

In most cases, the company will offer you their Licensing Agreement.  It's important to fully read and understand the contract before you sign it, if for no other reason to make certain that you're licensing your imagery and not selling                       it                       outright.

There's nothing wrong with selling all reproduction rights to an image as long as you're satisfied with the dollar compensation you receive.  The problem kicks in when you're talking about licensing and the company is talking about purchasing.  This difference in understanding often becomes apparent when their Assignment of Rights contract is presented.

You can get into trouble when the company has you sign an agreement which gives them all reproduction rights, now and in the future, to one of your images. That means that they--not you--own the art. Since they own your art they can use it for anything they want, resell it to another company, or license it to other companies for other uses for the next hundred years or so and you legally have absolutely no say in the matter.  You'll never make another cent from that image.

Owning all reproduction rights is generally what a

company means when they say they "buy all rights". This kind of arrangement works for illustrators and photographers who work on assignment and know full well that once they're paid by the client they'll never be able to use the art again. These folks generally understand what they're getting into when they sign a release. The problems kick in when an artist doesn't know what he or she is getting into.

The artist cannot rely on the friendliness of the people at the company and their verbal assurances. You certainly want an amiable working relationship with a client, but any verbal statement is negated once the contract is signed.

If you have any questions about the content of the contract and your rights and obligations once you've signed it, speak to an attorney. When they're in law school, attorneys learn about contracts and contract law, but without specific application to the fields of art and licensing. Make certain the attorney you're paying to review the contract has the necessary experience to recognize how certain key provisions of the agreement can affect your future ability to market your work.

The artist himself--and I cannot stress this enough--must read every line in the agreement himself and make sure he understands it. If you find that there are sections or sentences that aren't written clearly, don't say what you want, take away a bit more of your rights than you feel you want to give or if any of it seems confusing or contradictory, have the company rewrite it in plain English.

These are just a few of the examples of the kinds of things that companies insert into their contracts that the artist should be wary of:

1. The company gains the copyright for any of your pieces of art.
2. The company gains full and complete reproduction rights to any of your art.

3.  The company gains the right to sublicense your art to other companies without your having to approve and sign each specific sublicensing agreement.
4.  The company gains full ownership of your original works of art as part of the licensing agreement.

If the company isn't willing to rewrite the licensing contract to address these issues, then you may just want to think twice about what you're getting yourself into.

Don't let this kind of thing stop you from promoting your art for license. Most companies are reputable and most contracts are completely understandable by the average person. Just make sure you read every word, and know what it means.

Licensing contracts should always specify the length of time the license is for. And, it should address several issues that will present themselves at the end of the contract's term.

Reversionary rights are common in most license agreements, especially if the license has a fixed term of several years. Look for provisions entitled "Termination," "Term," "Reversion," "Grant of Rights," "Exploitation," or "Commercialization" to find reversionary rules. But be careful if a license agreement says it is "perpetual" or lasts "for the life of the copyright" or has similar language. There may not be any reversionary language and the agreement may not deal with the issue at all. This type of agreement would probably amount to an assignment of your rights, rather than a term of license.

When you locate language in a license agreement that describes a reversion, you need to determine the circumstances in which your rights would revert to you -- in other words, what has to happen in order for you to get the rights back. Ideally, you would want the rights to revert in the event that (1) the agreement terminates, (2) the company stops selling your work for a fixed period of time, (3) the company doesn't start selling your product by a certain date, or (4) the company materially breaches the agreement. It's pointless asking for reversion in the event that the company goes bankrupt because federal law usually prevents that from happening.

Foreign licensing of your artwork can also be lucrative, but it raises a number of additional concerns. When you allow a foreign company to license and sell your artwork as merchandise, the most important issue that arises has to do with people, not the contract. You can hire the world's most gifted lawyer to create a foreign licensing agreement, but if the other party is somewhat less than honest, or just inept, it doesn't matter what's printed on the agreement. You'll have to chase them into court in a foreign country and, assuming you win, you still have to collect your judgment before the licensee goes bankrupt or otherwise closes his doors.

When considering foreign licensing, start by asking two questions:

1. Has this company or person ever licensed artwork from a U.S. artist before? Don't be the first U.S. artist to deal with a foreign licensee. If a company has no experience with American licensors, you should have a strong reason to proceed with them, say, for example, the principals of the company are experienced in international licensing, although the company itself is new.

2. If the company has licensed artwork from U.S. artists, who are they and how can you contact them? Get the names and contact info for all of the artists who license with the foreign company, not just those recommended by the company. Find out whether those artists are satisfied with the company's quality, accounting, and general responsiveness.

Assuming you're satisfied that the company is reliable, you'll either be given a standard licensing agreement or you'll have to furnish one. In the case of foreign licenses, you're probably better off providing your own.

These are some of the important foreign licensing issues to keep in mind:

1.  Approval of licensed goods. It is reasonable to demand that copies of your licensed work be sent to you on a regular basis for approval. This offers you some assurance of consistency and quality for your work.

2.  Royalties and accounting. Payment of royalties from a foreign licensee can get tricky, especially when you consider issues like currency conversion rates, how the money will be paid, and what taxes may be applied against your sales or royalties. Before signing the license, inquire into national or local taxes that may apply. It's wise to include an audit provision which allows you to inspect the foreign licensee's books.

3.  Jurisdiction. Jurisdiction is the power of a court to bind the parties by its decision. Unless the company does substantial business in the states, the only way to get a foreign licensee into a U.S. court is to include a provision in the license agreement that requires the licensee to consent to U.S. jurisdiction.

4.  Choice of law. Every country--and every state-- has laws as to how contracts are interpreted. The licensee will want the disputes to be resolved under the laws of its country. Try to

include in your agreement that disputes will be resolved under U.S. law for copyright purposes and the laws of your state when it comes to contract issues.

5. Arbitration. Using arbitration, the parties hire a neutral arbitrator to evaluate the dispute and make a determination instead of filing a lawsuit. You'll almost always benefit by agreeing to have disputes arbitrated and inserting this into your agreement. If possible, your agreement should award attorney fees to the victor in the arbitration.

6. Foreign registrations. If your works are protected by U.S. intellectual property laws like copyright, you should determine whether it's worth your while to obtain foreign copyright in the countries where your work is being manufactured or distributed. You may be able to require that the licensee handle these administrative tasks as part of the license.

Until you've gone through the licensing process enough times to feel completely comfortable, consult a qualified attorney in every licensing instance. Failure to fully understand a legal agreement can result in a signed contract that obligates you to things you'd normally never even consider.

Contracts aside, it's important that you're comfortable with the people you're dealing with at the company, particularly if you're going to be responsible for producing variations on the image to customize its use, but don't allow a feeling of camaraderie to interfere with your ability to make prudent decisions. If in doubt, don't do the deal. Don't let your desire to earn royalties overcome your common sense.

Keep in mind that no license is probably better than a

bad license.

## A Promotional Gameplan

The first step in pursuing commercial work, whether that translates to garnering freelance assignments or selling licensing rights to imagery is to realistically inventory one's skills, interests and available artwork. The second step is volume.

Effective package design requires not only effective color coordination, but an appreciation for lettering and the ability to logically layout a bulk of type-faced information in an attractive manner. You'll need composition skills, of course, but you'll also need specific computer skills.

There are some 400 comic book titles published every month and a good many of those feature characters with capes and masks and more muscles than any three men could possibly build up no matter how many hours they spent at the gym. If you find the exciting exploits of The Masked Avenger somewhat less than fascinating, you probably shouldn't be pursuing an assignment to ink the next issue.

Heroic Fantasy has always appealed to you, and the Gaming publishers are always on the lookout for new talent. The specs are pretty cut and dry, however, and what they require is detailed renditions of Fantasy figures. Your current portfolio reflects good drawing ability, but mostly cuddly cartoon figures. This is not the time to approach this market.

Many artists set themselves up for failure in two ways: they either approach a potential client with inappropriate material, or they simply don't approach enough potential clients.

Determine those areas in which your style might be appropriate. No one can do this for you and if you aren't realistic you're setting yourself up for a lot of wasted postage. Desire simply isn't enough. If your skill level needs improving, take the steps to upgrade your skills.

Determine those areas you'd like to produce work for. Then, do it. A minimum of six professional samples for each arena you choose to pursue, every sample rendered to the best of your ability. Six exceptional samples of your work in any given genre is an adequate representation of your skills and an adequate representation of your commitment to a given genre. Secure good reproductions of the originals and assemble submission packages. I say packages because--for example-- you'll have one package you submit to comic book publishers and another you submit to coloring book publishers.

Determine those particular markets you wish to pursue. The best sources for identification are arguably The Artists' Market and the Advertiser's Index.

Make certain that your submission packages announce your professionalism. Enclose a self-addressed stamped envelope.

Then, submit.

At a minimum, the beginning artist should submit ten, count 'em, ten packages each and every week. You've got to identify those art directors who appreciate your technique and the more of them that see your work the sooner you'll find each other.

As time goes by and assignments begin to trickle in, you'll develop a client list, a list of art directors you'll regularly contact and who will regularly contact you when assignments are available. As your client list becomes more extensive, you'll probably cut down on the number of sample packages you put out, but until that happens you want to send out those ten packages each and every week including Christmas and your birthday.

If you're chasing licensing as well as outright assignment, add licensing packages to your total, don't subtract them, i.e., ten submission packages plus two licensing packages. Licensing packages need to be tailored for each individual market you send them to.  Submission packages just need to be copied.

Practice your skills, develop your own personal style and put your work out there.

## The Artist as Entrepreneur

### The Art of Business vs. the Business of Art

Traditionally, the artist has depended on existing publishing entities to purchase, reproduce and distribute his work, has depended on existing entities to generate his income and in the process has traded his efforts for inevitably lower returns than might have been expected. This holds true regardless of the venue the artist chose to pursue, whether selling self-generated imagery or chasing illustration assignments.

There are hundreds, perhaps thousands of publishing avenues available to the artist that are fair and competent and smart enough to realize that the welfare of the artist--in effect their supplier--directly relates to the quality and the quantity of work that artist will make available to them and behave accordingly, but even those publishing entities must generate an internal profit to survive. That profit is secured by retaining a healthy portion of the sales money generated by the artist's endeavors.

Thanks to the advancement of communication and printing technologies, opportunities for entrepreneurial activity, specifically self-publication and distribution, are now often a viable alternative for the working artist.

Delving into the entrepreneurial pool isn't for everybody. There are certainly added expectations of return on production, but there are also added responsibilities and the necessity of assuming the mantle of the businessman in addition to that of the artist. The artist who cannot separate his emotions from his finished work will ultimately garner little success as an entrepreneur. On the other hand, the artist who can focus his emotion on creating, then shield himself from emotional attachment and find some objectivity--in other words, view the work as a product-- can do well.

Self-publication is no easy task. Not only is the artist the creator of an image, he is now the production manager, promotions manager and sales manager, not to mention accountant and shipping clerk. In short, the artist has formed a small company and is now a businessman.

This prospect will have little appeal for many creative people. Those individuals who relish the notion of control will embrace this concept more readily. And do not make the mistake of assuming that publishing your own work means that the standards are somehow reduced from those of other publishers. The fact is if your work couldn't sell to an existing greeting card company it isn't likely to generate sales because you've published it yourself.

The artist who would be an Entrepreneur must master four operational components:

*Concept*
*Creation*
*Marketing*
*Sales*

Artists tend to focus their efforts on Concept and Creation. Most prefer to leave Marketing and Sales in the hands of others or sometimes just to providence. The successful entrepreneur must be willing, even eager to devote time and resources to the full spectrum of running his business. If he sees Concept and Creation as the only significant activity in his daily routine, if Marketing and Sales are measures in which he has little to no interest and less commitment to the proper functioning of, the artist is best served by a rapid retreat from the concept of independent publication and should instead continue presenting his work to existing publishers in the best light possible.

Generally speaking, the potential for greater personal

financial return on one's creative efforts is more likely when the artist controls his handiwork than when that handiwork is simply placed in another's trust, assuming the artist has indeed produced imagery that has a certain mass appeal and that the artist is willing to undertake the sometimes monumental task of reproducing and promoting the work.

There are only three reasons why artists fail in the art publishing business:

1. **The product simply isn't viable.** There's something about the product that doesn't work--the quality of the reproductions are amateurish, the price point is inappropriate or the work itself just doesn't have enough mass appeal to generate a decent return on marketing efforts.

2. **Sales and marketing efforts are ineffective.** The work certainly has the potential to successfully compete in the marketplace, but sales and marketing efforts are sabotaged by approaching the wrong clients in the wrong way.

3. **The artist doesn't understand that starting and running a business is a job.** I talk with a lot of people who spend less than twenty hours a week trying to build a viable operation and don't understand why they can't make a living in the art publishing business--and often, those twenty hours actually includes time spent on Concept and Creation.

**Product, Product, Product**

Let's assume for a moment that the artist decides to enter the poster market. This is a logical first step toward self-publishing because the imagery is readily available and the selling avenues are easily accessible. It's not uncommon for poster publishing houses to offer a flat $1000 fee for the right to produce unlimited copies of an image in poster format. Often, that price includes their acquisition of the original art.

Now, let's approach poster publication for another avenue.

You've sold your 18" x 24" original painting for $1,000. Printing three hundred and fifty 18" x 24" reproductions on 100-pound gloss stock will currently cost approximately $750. This translates to a cost per reproduction of $2.50.

For the sake of argument, let's agree to designate the first fifty reproductions as a signed and numbered limited edition. We'll agree that these signed and numbered prints will sell for $100 each. The remaining two-hundred seventy five reproductions will be sold as posters, retail price $30. We'll assume that one-hundred will be sold directly to the consumer (either directly from your studio or from your website or at street fairs) and that two hundred will be wholesaled to print shops and picture framing stores (standard wholesale is 50% of the retail price, or in this case $15 per reproduction).

Here's how it all translates:

**Signed & Numbered Edition of 50 @ $100 each**    **$ 5,000.00**
**Retail of 100 reproductions @ $30 each**    **$3,000.00**
**Wholesale of 200 reproductions @ $15 each**    **$3,000.00**
**Total sales of reproductions**    **$11,000.00**

In the lucky event that the reproduced image becomes a popular one, you are certainly able to reprint the poster edition, gaining additional income from the image.

And, note that this dollar amount is in addition to the $1000 purchase price paid for the original artwork.

The artist must be prudent in his selection of what work to reproduce. Not every image has the potential to generate volume sales of reproductions to justify the investment in printing. Selection becomes less of a decision about aesthetics and more of a decision about viability in the marketplace.

The entrepreneur must study those areas in which he wishes to emerge. Poster publishing is a good first step because selling avenues are readily available to the artist. Private exhibitions, sales from the studio, street fairs, art festivals and the artist's website are easily accessed avenues to present the product to potential buyers. Additionally, most picture framing shops sell posters as well and the artist may well be able to wholesale product to these shops, either by selling to them directly or via partnership with an independent sales representative or distributor.

Greeting cards are another easily accessible market. Much of the imagery that will sell as posters will sell as greeting cards. Advanced printing technology makes it possible to print greeting cards from a personal computer in the studio as the orders come in, negating the necessity of investing large sums of money into securing stock. As sales figures increase and popular imagery is identified, particular images can be commercially printed when it's viable to do so.

Mary Englebreit and Jody Bergsma are prime examples of the possibilities inherent in self-publication. Ms. Engelbreit has created a small empire with her images of homespun humor and reflection, everything from greeting cards and notepads to tin boxes and even a slick monthly magazine. Ms. Bergsma began with a series of whimsical images that evolved into a series of mystical and sometimes spiritual interpretations featured on greeting cards, posters, fine art prints and even published in book form. Ms. Bergsma owns her own gallery as well.

Neither Mary Englebreit nor Jody Bergsma entered the

world of self-publishing or achieved success in the publishing field because of a lack of interest in their work by other publishing concerns. Their imagery caught the public's attention and both women had the courage to assume control over their output and their income.

The entrepreneur may well find that the artist himself is as an important factor in determining success as the artist's work.

Todd McFarlane began as a talented comic book artist and eventually wound up with a steady assignment to produce the art for Marvel's Spider-Man, an assignment most in the comics industry would have considered the top of the comic book heap. McFarlane had other ambitions, however, and eventually dropped the Marvel assignment to pursue self-publishing Spawn, a character he himself created. Spawn became a phenomenally successful independent comic book, even became a series of motion pictures starring Wesley Snipes as the main character. McFarlane parlayed that success into his own publishing empire, an empire which now includes a toy manufacturing and distributing operation. While his illustrating skills played an essential part in his success, a personality designed to embrace and pursue the business aspect of creation led him to ultimate success. Todd McFarlane is as important a player in the comic industry as any of his creations.

If the entrepreneur is to be successful, the business must become as important to him as the creation of the work. The artist will need to acquire additional business skills, will need coaching in the art of marketing, will need to recognize the importance of accounting and be willing to devote the appropriate amount of time to mastering all.

If the artist's interests are truly planted only in creation, he will do better to simply create to the best of his ability and leave publishing and promotion to other entities. If on the other hand the artist is willing to gleefully embrace the opportunity to obtain and apply a new set of skills, the potential return can be extraordinary.

### Establish a Corporate Image

Every successful corporate entity owes its success, in part, to a carefully cultivated recognition factor. We know what Dr. Pepper is, we recognize Playskool. The artist who would become an entrepreneurial success must begin by establishing a corporate identity.

Barry Moser became a success self-publishing retold versions of classics in book form, including Alice in Wonderland, Frankenstein, Dracula and even a version of the Holy Bible. His Pennywhistle Press is known throughout the book industry as a publisher of fine collectable volumes. Book dealer remember Pennywhistle even if they can't quite remember Barry Moser.

Real Musgrave is an easy enough name to remember, but Pocket Dragons is even easier. Musgrave produces and distributes his whimsical creations as posters and greeting cards, and licensed as embellishment on any number of products (cups, plates, bookmarks, t-shirts, statuettes).

Wendy and Richard Pini produced one of the first commercially successful independent comic books. They called the book Elfquest, but they formed a company called Warp Graphics to publish the book and market subsidiary rights.

Establishing a corporate image allows the entrepreneur to discard product that simply doesn't do well while adding product with potential without sacrificing the goodwill he's built among both the general public and his customer base.

The first thing an entrepreneur must do is to choose an appropriate name for his business operation and design a logo. Then, the artist must begin to think in corporate terms of selling his work instead of personal terms.

**Creation, Production, Promotion & Sales**

A product-based business is concerned with four major functions: Creation, Production, Promotion and Sales.

Creation is the process of conception and initial execution of a product idea. The artist, for example, creates a painting he believes is potentially a best-selling poster.

Production is the process of manufacturing the product that will be eventually find its way into the hands of the consumer. Continuing with the idea of a poster, this means contracting with a printer to produce a given number of copies printed to the exact specifications of the artist.

Promotion is the process of informing the buying public that the image is available for purchase. This is accomplished in any number of ways, everything from exhibiting the final product at Street Fairs to displaying the product on the artist's website to purchasing advertising space in trade journals and consumer publications.

Sales is the act of exchanging product for monetary consideration. Your idea has been converted into a manufactured product and brought to the attention of someone who paid you money for it.

Business, especially the art business, is not an especially complicated process. Each of these four factions--creation, production, promotion and sales--has the potential to become time-consuming and to demand extraordinary attention to detail, but the process itself if clear-cut and simple. That said, the entrepreneur who is lacking in the ability to adequately diversify his activity focus or who has particular problems with time management may become overwhelmed.

**Publishing & Private Label Product Manufacturing**

At the very least, the artist should consider private label publishing.

There are any number of online companies, such as Cafe

Press, which will take the artist's work and reproduce it on posters, greeting cards and various other products on-demand. The artist contracts with the company, delivers the art--usually via computer--the company takes the order and the payment, produces the product, ships the order and pays the artist. There is usually no cost to the artist for setup.

The artist is generally responsible for promotion, i.e., directing customers to the site displaying his art, but a good return on effort is possible.

## Profit & Loss

As a business person, your primary concern becomes Profit and Loss, in other words did you total conception, production, marketing and sales activity produce a monetary gain or a monetary loss.

It is most heartily recommended that if the artist is seriously considering the reproduction and distribution of his own work, no matter what format he considers appropriate, that he spend some time involved in exploration of the basic principles of business. An understanding of basic sales technique and basic accounting principles will go a long way toward helping the artist turned entrepreneur employ his talent to create a continuing income.

### Publishing Your Own Work

There is no magic to achieving a lucrative career in the Art Publishing industry, no one particular thing that will guarantee success. Instead, the self-publisher must become competent in a variety of different areas and pursue each with unlimited persistence.

We will explore those areas important to securing a lucrative and continuing career as an art publisher. We will discuss promotion, sales and marketing--as pertaining to the art publishing industry--and subsidiary marketing--sometimes referred to as Licensing--and we will detail how to identify and approach those potential clients. We will assume you'll be publishing and licensing your own work, so it will not deal with the process and problems involved in acquired images you don't own.

The manual will suggest methods of effectively showcasing your product to individual consumers, retailers, distributors, trade shows, and street fairs and festivals. An Addendum includes examples of various promotional items, introductory sales letters and telephone scripts for use in following up with potential customers. We will demonstrate how to tie your hard-copy promotional efforts to your website and greatly increase the opportunities for repeat business. You'll learn to think "outside the box" and approach categories of potential customers you might not normally consider.

We will assemble a plan of attack to get your product in front of the right people and help those people decide to buy.

We'll discuss the business aspects of production and distribution, and the copyright and trademark aspects of the art publishing business.

Finally, we will develop a schedule to encompass not only your marketing efforts, but your creative efforts as well--you don't want to lose ground when your line begins to take off because you've neglected offering fresh imagery.

This seminar does not deal specifically with the creative aspects of originating your product. I assume you've got a pretty good idea of what you want to produce at this point.    The successful self-publishing entrepreneur is a hybrid of artist and businessperson, a merge of two factions often at odds. Like nitroglycerin, the mixture can be perilous. Properly applied, it can explode the restraints that prevent personal accomplishment.

E.B. White is generally regarded as one of the most effective communicators ever to put pen to paper. His prose is direct, expressive and efficient.  His masterpiece Charlotte's Web, a favorite with children, and The Elements of Style, a volume on composition that Mr. White shares authorship with William Strunk, Jr., are each in their own right classics.

The simple truth is that no one would have much cared about Mr. White's verbal functionality if he hadn't had absolutely enchanting things to tell us.

The same simple truth applies to the product you produce. Good marketing habits and effective sales presentation abilities are extraordinary tools, but those tools are completely useless if you're trying to convince a potential customer to invest in a product that is poorly conceived, shoddily rendered, badly reproduced and chaotically packaged.  The first and most important key to success in the Art Publishing Business is the ability to set aside one's artistic ego and consider the rendered art as a viable product.

The self-publisher must make a clear determination as to the marketing viability of his or her product because that viability is what determines whether or not a particular design will sell.  This isn't meant to imply that the only means to success is to mimic products already on the card shelves, but it does mean that if the new product is considerably different from what the buyer might expect the self-publisher had better be prepared to look a lot longer and a lot harder to find someone to purchase his wares.

From a business perspective, the artist must choose a method of production that allows timely delivery to clients. Production questions should be asked and answered well before a catalog is put in front of a potential customer. The time to decide that hand-painting designs preprinted on cardstock is too time-consuming to allow for a reasonable delivery turn-around time is before the order is placed, not after the order is asked for. A new vendor gets one change to impress a new client with his professionalism, and generally only one chance. Professionals rarely prefer dealing with Amateurs.

The self-publisher needs to explore the total spectrum of product options. Handmade products are usually more expensive and are purchased by collectors, but often a less expensive mass produced reproduction of that design will do quite well in a general retail environment. A dual publishing effort has an enormous potential to increase profit margin, but the effort involved in pursuing a dual market also has the potential to tie up a great deal of the self-publisher's time, both in terms of production and in terms of marketing and distribution. And, if the design will be sold as a reproduction, what method of printing is to be used? Thankfully, printing technology has reached a point where cost is less of an impediment than it once was for the independent publisher.

And, whatever production decisions are instigated, product quality becomes a most important issue. A major selling point of dealing with an independent self-publishing creator, other than the option of acquiring a more unique product, is the quality of that product. As a self-publisher, your name is not only on the original art, it's printed across the reproduced product as well.

## Pricing for Profit, Not Loss

It is important to know exactly how much it costs you to

produce your individual product. There are variables, depending on the particular formula you choose to determine profit and loss. Your particular formula may include built-in compensation for time spent creating the original product. Or not. It should include promotional costs--after paper supplies and printing costs, promotion will probably be your biggest expense.

Initial success, assuming a viable product, strongly depends on competitive pricing. It isn't necessary to undercut the competition's price, but you don't want a price point considerably above the average, either.

If you're selling directly to consumers, you'll charge a set price. If you're wholesaling to retailers, you'll generally charge 50% of that price. If you're working with a distributor to get your product into store, he'll usually charge 15-20% of the wholesale price.

Individual item cost is the primary factor you'll use in determining most production issues. Spend some time researching product that is similar to your own and determine a reasonable selling price for your own product. Then, begin exploring methods of minimizing your production costs.

The goal of the self-publisher is profit, and the only way to determine profit is to subtract expenses from income. There is nothing more exasperating than having what appears to have been a successful selling year only to have your accountant explain that your profit margin for that fiscal period is almost enough to cover dinner and a movie.

**Production, Production, Production**

Variety is one of the most important assets available to the self-publishing entrepreneur. Regardless of whether your focus is selling to individual consumers at craft fairs or retailers or just to anyone with a few extra bucks via the Internet, you'll need a variety of designs in order to build an effective display.

Recommendations vary as to an appropriate number of

designs.    Individual consumers may not be hesitant about purchasing if you've only got half-a-dozen choices, but retailers want to be assured that if they take a chance on your product, and if that product indeed sells for them, that you're going to be around for them to reorder.  The simplest way to moderate those concerns is to have a solid variety of designed product available. You've got to have enough product available to demonstrate to a potential client that you're in it for the long haul and that you are a vendor he can depend upon for ongoing inventory.

Not to mention the fact that mathematically speaking, the more product you have to offer the greater the possibility of selling some of that product.

Okay.   You've got a pretty good idea of what your product is going to be.  You've figured out what you want to produce and how you want it to look.

Now is the time to step back and make certain that the product you have in mind is a product that you not only believe in, but is a product that you can realistically see sitting in a card rack at your local Greeting Card store or in the poster bin at your local Picture Framing shop.  It isn't necessary that your subject matter and artistic style possess some mystical universal appeal, but it is necessary that the product you want to sell has a professional appearance--dynamic conception, skilled rendering, quality reproduction and appropriate packaging.

And so, armed with a quality product and a burning desire for financial success, we  move to Step Two.

## Writing a Tailored Business Plan

Greeting Card industry estimates show that more than eight billion greeting cards were sold to Americans last year-- which breaks down to about 250 cards sold per second!

Art Reproductions--posters--are selling stronger than ever, bolstered by the Internet and the fact that good imagery requires no foreign language skills to appreciate.

Comic Books are flourishing. There are currently more than four-hundred titles available generating dollars not only from sales of the books themselves, but from licensing projects ranging from action figures to big-budget movie adaptations.

Further good news is that almost half of these products are created and sold by independent creators. If you have a talent for drawing, painting, or cartooning and the gumption to make sure your creative efforts find their way to someplace a potential customer might conceivably find them, there's a better than even chance you can make a success of this business.

As an entrepreneur you'll need to devise a business plan to map the course you'll follow in your day-day-operation. There are two types of business plans.

The first is the financial document assembled in preparation for a business loan conference or to entice investors. This document is best discussed with your accountant and your attorney, and I strongly suggest that if securing a business loan-- other than the use of a MasterCard or Visa, which incidentally is the method most often used in America by small business entrepreneurs to finance their business startup--or finding investors is important to you, then by all means secure recommendations from someone you trust and proceed accordingly.

We shall focus on the second variety. The second type of business plan is a personal roadmap you assemble that clearly shows a definite route to follow to reach your destination: success. The bank won't be much interested in this one. It details not only your Product Line, but your Strengths and Weaknesses in areas you wouldn't dare discuss with a financial investor. It clearly delineates your total responsibilities, not only as pertaining to your new Greeting Card Business, but in other seemingly unrelated areas both personal and private. It outlines the criteria by which you'll gauge your progress or lack thereof. It requires an honest consideration of your hopes and dreams and even your talent. Depending on your personal penchant for detail, this can be an exasperatingly complicated document.

Construction of a viable business plan requires you to truthfully answer three questions:

    1. What exactly is it that I want?
    2. What do I have to do to get what I want?
    3. Is doing what I have to do to get what I think I want really worth the trouble?

I sincerely belief the reason most small businesses fail is because the entrepreneur neglected full consideration of Question Number Three.

## The Artist vs. the Entrepreneur

As your own boss, you have total control over what you want to create. No guidelines to adhere to, no editor to follow, and no bureaucracy to go along with, but there is one important drawback: you are not focused solely on the creation aspect. You need to take care of the supply chain, production, financing, marketing, selling, bookkeeping and administrative tasks. This process is generally exhilarating to the Entrepreneur and exasperating to the Artist.

Most creative people don't decide to purse a creative career so they can spend half their time involved in administrative, production and promotional tasks. It's important to strike a balance between the two. You want to schedule your activity so that you're as productive as possible on the business end without dampening your enthusiasm for the creative process.

A recent survey suggested that even the most productive people working in a corporate office are actively involved in actually doing their job a little less than five hours a day no matter how many hours they spend in the office. The rest of the day is interruptions, chit-chat, personal business and breaks. If you're determined to successfully combine a personal business operation with your creative endeavors, you need to learn how to focus on what's truly productive and ignore the chatter.

## One Size Doesn't Fit All

In order to write an effective individualized business plan, you have to decide exactly what your initial product offering will be. You can amend that product later, but you have to have one to start with. Your concerns will be unique to your situation and as such a cookie cutter business plan will do you little to no good. Indeed, it may actually hurt you in the long run.

There are a wide variety of variables that must be included to make your plan a valid one. Production costs will vary thanks to different design factors. If your products are handmade, you're dealing with the cost of raw materials. If your products are to be reproduced, you're dealing with the cost of raw materials as well as the cost of whatever printing method you decide upon. If you decide on commercial printing, you'll need to include shipping and possible storage consideration. You'll need to stock the proper sized envelopes and mailing boxes.

If you've decided your product would do well in a festival environment and decided to play the street fair circuit, you'll need display racks, a table and comfortable portable chair. You'll also need a dependable method of transportation to cart these things to the affair

You'll need to think about financing. Starting an art publishing business is considerably less expensive than buying a McDonald's franchise and a lot less fattening, but there are expenses involved and it will take time to begin generating any dollar volume, much less any that could conceivably be considered profit--which means you'll need to think about living expenses and devise some method of supporting yourself while you're building your business.

And, you'll need to sketch out both a short-range and a long-range plan of action. What shape do you want your business to be in six months from now? A year from now? Three years from now?

What are you prepared to do to get it there? And what are you not prepared to do?

**Role Model, Not Role Playing**

The only justification for being in business is to generate profit. You may produce art to satisfy your creative urges, but the moment you've signed your name to the piece it must be viewed as a product, and exchanging that product for cold, hard cash is the only rationale for enduring the frustration that comes with the daily operation of any business entity. Well, that and avoiding the necessity of a part-time career in food service.

We are fortunate in that others have gone before us. They might not have proven what will work for us individually, but they have documented most of the aspects of the art publishing business that will make achieving success a somewhat easier chore. Study the

There is a certain charm connected to doing business directly with the artist. It is perceived that there is more certainty in doing business with a businessperson. Learn to separate the creative aspect of your personality from the entrepreneurial side of your personality. Don't abandon either one of them, just learn when to show which and when to show a little of both.

**Your Hopes, Your Dreams, Your Plans and Your Finances**

Chances are you became an artist because the idea of

creation fascinated you. Some inwardly driven force compelled you to pick up a pencil or a brush or a camera or paper and scraps of glue and apply your most concentrated efforts.

And every artist I've ever spoken with wants to sell enough of his artwork to support him or herself. It's only reasonable to hope to make a living doing the thing you love the most.

Artists tend to speak in terms of inspiration when it comes to creation. That's all well and good, but there's a little voice that squeaks between my ears insisting that inspiration is little more than unfocused observation. If you're going to assume the responsibility for proactively selling enough of your work to allow you to devote your full efforts to producing more of it, it's important to remember that the day comes and the day goes and those who wait for inspiration to spur them into action are generally found game shows on one of the television cable networks.

Good time management is of the utmost importance. Your working time must be scheduled. Yes, as a self-employed, budding business mogul you certainly have the final say in determining just how flexible you'll be with the time you have available, but the business aspect of your dual career is at least as important as the creative aspect and if you're anything like the rest of us, especially those of us with a creative bent, it's very easy to let the time you meant to spend on business slip away while you toil away on the next masterpiece. There's the suggestion that you can plan to win or you can plan to fail; not planning or failing to follow your plan is simply planning to fail.

Dedicate a specific period of time each day to just the business aspect of your career. In the beginning, you'll need time to assemble promotional packages and make telephone calls. As those efforts result in orders, you'll need time to reproduce, package and ship them, but you'll still need the time to handle promotion. As you begin to see more results from your promotional activity--and you will see results if you're both consistent and persistent--you'll need even more time to get the product out to your customers.  With luck, you'll reach a point where your business efforts are eating up so much of your time you begin to worry about the amount of creation time you have available.  At that point, you'll hopefully be able to afford to hire someone to handle those monotonous little details--like folding cards and packaging promotional material--that don't absolutely require your hands-on expertise.

Someone once defined an entrepreneur as someone willing to work eighty hours a week for himself so he didn't have to work forty hours a week for someone else.  The upside of it is that the entrepreneur is the one who benefits financially from his efforts.

No one believes in a product that has no value, not even the person who created it.  If you believe in your product and you believe in your talent, the very least you can do is give yourself the opportunity to benefit financially from your talents.

## A Realistic Game Plan for Success

Success in any endeavor that involves selling a product requires recognition of the "numbers factor".   The more people who see your product, the greater the chances are of finding someone who wishes to purchase your product.

Statistically, the best chance for continuing financial success is getting your cards into the retail stores.  It doesn't matter whether you're selling an original hand-made product or a quality reproduction, you've got a much better chance of exposing your cards to the greatest number of people in an atmosphere that is more exclusively conducive to buying than any other venue.  Street Fairs and Craft Shows can certainly result in additional income, and are a terrific promotional gambit, but a retail environment showcases your product day in and day out.  And, since that retail environment is your best bet, you'll want to put your product into as many retail stores as possible.

You'll want to pursue Distributors to handle your product, but you don't necessarily want to wait for them to produce.  You may also find that Distributors are more interested in carrying a product that has already proven its viability in the marketplace, so if you've got product in some stores you'll having an easier time signing a Distributor.

At a minimum, your promotional efforts should include ten sales packages mailed to retailers each and every week.  That means you'll schedule ten follow-up sales calls for the following week.

At a minimum, your promotional efforts should include five sales packages mailed to distributors each and every week.  That means you'll schedule an additional five follow-up sales calls for the following week.

You should contact retailers who become customers once a month to introduce new product and solicit new orders.

Get used to the concept of rejection.  It isn't personal and it isn't even necessarily a reaction to the quality of the work your produce.  Retailer and distributors are in business to generate profit and both will readily acquire whatever new product they think will appeal to their customer base.  It may just be that your product isn't seen as something their existing customers will embrace.

Or, they just might not like your stuff.  People are human and knee-jerk reactions are common.

That's okay, too.  If people didn't have different preferences the opportunity for success in the art publishing business would be non-existent.

Somewhere in that crowd of potential customers out there are the ones who will find your particular product enchanting, will place an initial order, display your product to best advantage and reorder when those are gone.  The trick is to identify them.

And the only way to do it is pick a starting spot in the crowd and start asking. Every one of them who tells you "NO" brings you one step closer to finding the ones you're looking for.

The more people you ask everyday, the more quickly you'll find the ones you're looking for.

## Promoting Your Business

Hopefully, growing your company will be an enjoyable endeavor. The work will become even more enjoyable as your success begins to flourish, but for that to happen your newly born art publishing company must be perceived as stable and professional.

It's time to become a brand name: *name your company.*

Those three little words have probably shot an extra pint of adrenaline into your bloodstream and at this moment swirls of verbiage flurry behind your eyes and between your ears as you consider the possibilities.

The company name should be easy to remember.

It should be a name you're comfortable with because if you're diligent and persistent and even just a little bit lucky you're going to be stuck with that name for a long, long time.

It should be a name that doesn't immediately remind people of another company, especially one that produces a product similar to your own, and it wouldn't hurt if the name were fairly easy to pronounce.

One big reason Hallmark became so successful is that they wisely chose to promote their name as opposed to just promoting their product. They've plastered that name on the back of every card they've ever printed, on every paper bag they could get their hands on, on every storefront they could rent space for, and now even on cable television with a network promoting family programming sponsored by Hallmark. The result? Mention the term "greeting card" in a room of a hundred people and better than 90% of them will momentarily think "Hallmark".

Being to think in terms of BRAND.

Products change. New designs are added, designs that didn't sell well are dropped. The designs you're selling today will probably not be the designs you're selling a year from now.

People like something new and make purchase decisions accordingly, and it's up to you to make sure that what you offer is fresh and exciting.  At the same time, it's important that your customers have a frame of reference in which to remember the kind of product you produce.

Mary Englebreit may have started her career as an anonymous freelance illustrator and designer, but her entrepreneurial nature helped her name evolve into a brand.  Ms. Englebreit's distinctive style certainly catches one's attention and her "ME" logo immediately gives her customers a frame of reference in which to search for new imagery.

Real Musgrave is a name that might be easy enough to remember, but the brand name Pocket Dragons is a name almost impossible to forget.  Musgrave's floppy-eared dragonette logo has actually generated income as a stand-alone entity, appearing first as a poster, then a t-shirt design and finally as a desk-top statue.

It's important to promote your product, but it's just as important to promote your brand.  Customers will usually remember your brand name before they remember your name, so it's important to use your brand name prominently on every product and every piece of promotion you produce.

Now, *design a Logo* and make sure to print it on the back of each and every one of the cards your release.

### The Business Card and the Product Catalog

A Business Card has a single purpose:  to archive contact information in a convenient and easily retrievable manner.

A Product Catalog has a different, but still solitary purpose:  to archive product information in a convenient and easily retrievable manner.

Of course you'll want to design both your business card and your product catalog with an eye toward reflecting the individuality of the product you offer, but it is essential that design aesthetics do not interfere with that solitary purpose so desperately necessary for your business to succeed.

Potential customers won't generally take the time to find a magnifying glass so they can read the phone number printed in tiny, little letters and folded beneath a reproduction of a greeting card that probably lost most of its definition in the reduced printed size. Likewise, a potential customer won't take the time to consider that the color printing in your catalog dulls because of the cheap newsprint you chose to put between the covers and that your actual product has a more appealing brightness.

Clichés are clichés because they're generally true. Well, and convenient. What I'm getting at here is the fact that you get one chance to make a first impression: just one. This is especially true if that impression comes out of a mailed promotional package.

If you're on the premises, your business card and your product catalog introduce you, and you want to make certain that you're introduced as a professional, not some sort of weekend hobbyist or rank amateur.

If you're not on the premises, your business card and your product catalog are you, and they'd better introduce you as a professional or they'll wind up unread and pitched into that small metal can generally kept next to a desk or under a cash register.

## Identifying Your Marketplace

The logical first assumption is that if you're going into the art publishing business the most appropriate outlet for your product is a retailer. That might not be the case.

If you're producing a more-or-less traditional product, the retailer is certainly a good place to start, but if you're product is designed to appeal to other than the traditional customer you'll need to pursue directed outlets for your products.

For example, if you're producing detailed art featuring a variety of watercraft--boats, ships, barges--you'll want to pursue those retailers whose businesses attract the kind of customer who is interested in watercraft. You'd contact all the chandler shops, especially those specializing in recreational equipment, as well as the traditional retailer. You'd consider renting booth space at this year's Boat Show. You'd contact distributing firms who handle the kind of product that requires them to call on chandlers and recreation concerns. You'd talk to a few Yacht Brokers, who with luck would either want to put a rack of cards in their showroom or perhaps purchase a block of your product for themselves to use as promotional material.

And you'd still pursue traditional retailers.

## Promotion, Promotion, Promotion

There is no one big promotional idea guaranteed to make your product sell.

Your chances of selling improves every time someone looks at your product. Effective promotion is a circle of activity with everything working in tandem. Your logo reminds people of your brand name which reminds them of the particular kind of product you offer. Your business card works in harmony with your product catalog and your web site to direct the customer to a place where a decision to purchase is possible. Even your products are part of that promotional circle, directing the buyer to your web site for a chance to be seduced by your other offerings.

Promotion never ends. It's something you must do every day, day in and day out, and on those rare days when you aren't actively promoting your product it'll probably be because you're developing a new approach to present your product to the world.

When it's all said and done, that's what promotion is: putting your product information in the hands of someone who just might be interested in buying. If that doesn't happen, and happen often, your company is doomed.        The Functional Art of Sales & Marketing

There are a half-a-dozen accurate ways to define Sales and Marketing. It depends on whom you find yourself speaking to and the nuance of your conversation.

I like things simple and direct:

> Sales and Marketing is the Art of presenting your product to a potential buyer in a way that makes it not only prudent, but convenient for him to purchase, and then asking that buyer to purchase again and again and again.

There are literally hundreds of books on mastering the art of selling. If you've learned the concept of talking to people instead of at them you may find it unnecessary to purchase any of those volumes..

There are four simple concepts I try to remember in a sales situation. If you'll remember these principles, you'll not only wind up placing more product, you'll do it with a lot less stress.

1. I expect to be treated as an adult by the people I choose to deal with. I have a sneaking suspicion everybody else pretty much appreciates the same consideration. Somebody who doesn't care for your product won't usually buy it just because they like you, but people who do care for your product--but don't much care for you-- well, they probably won't buy it, either.

2. Everyone I deal with is at least as smart as I am...whether they are or not. Everyone I speak with is my equal. The moment I realize my conversation even hints at condescension that

conversation is finished.

3.  A sales conversation is just that--a conversation. The point of the conversation is to present my work to someone who isn't familiar with it and receive feedback, hopefully positive, but probably useful either way. If the feedback is positive I know there's a pretty good chance of putting my product into that store. If the feedback is negative, it's probably not going to happen, but I'm smart enough to accept that the product has been rejected, not the artist. And, I'm smart enough to move on to the next store.

4.  You can't talk people into buying what they don't want. Yes, I can probably trick or guilt someone into signing a small initial order, but the key to success isn't one order--it's one order over and over and over. The prospect who doesn't particularly care for my product is a prospect I'm better off not partnering with...which, incidentally, doesn't mean I'm not going to ask what it is about the product that makes this particular prospect think it's not viable.

Sales and Marketing is part of the job. It may not be your favorite part, and that's okay, but it is a big part of what will bring you success in the business world. If it isn't possible for you to develop a willingness to open yourself up on a regular basis and talk in a warm, friendly manner to a bunch of people you don't know, then you've probably chosen the wrong method of chasing success as an artist.

There are a variety of ways to market your product and we'll look at several of those which have proven successful, but a face to face introduction to your product will always result in more product placement--sales--than any other method.

## Position Your Product

You'll want to make certain that anyone with an interest in the kind of product you produce or its subject matter has the best opportunity to stumble across it.

To do this effectively, you first have to identify those people who might have an interest in your product. If you're publishing baby birth announcements, you'll want to approach traditional greeting card retailers, but you'll also want to approach maternity clothing stores, children's book stores and probably even a few toy shops.

Where are people who might be interested in birth announcement (or ships or carousel horses or bikini-clad redheads) likely to be? That's where you need to place your product.

## Approach & Conquer: Seduction of the Not-So-Innocent

You want to make a good first impression--it's important that you are perceived as a professional when you approach a potential client, especially if that contact is via mailed printed material. Your printed material must present a professional image.

And so should you. If you're physically calling on a prospect, whether you're carting your sample case into a retail store or meeting a potential distributor for a cup of coffee and a chat, make sure you've put yourself together in such a way that it's obvious the encounter is important to you. The art publishing business is considerably less formal than, say, the pharmaceutical business, but in both you're asking someone you don't know to invest in you, your product and your company. The suit you wear to weddings and funerals can probably stay in the closet, but the jeans and sneakers probably need to stay in there with them. Remember, you're a business professional whose product happens to be a creative one, not a creative person who's hoping that the business world will take you seriously.

Present a successful business image. People generally tend to believe what they see until they've been given a reason not to.

## The Sales Package

My initial contact with Retailers and Distributors is a "one sheet promo". I designed the sheet from scratch using Microsoft Word--you can do wondrous things if you're willing to learn to play with the TEXT BOX function--and in a pinch the sheet reproduces well on an inkjet color printer using 110-pound Bright White Cardstock. If you can design a card or a poster--in fact, any published art product--you can design a catalog page. Hiring a marketing firm to design it for you is a horrendous waste of money.

Printing bound catalogs, at least in the early days of your distribution efforts, is probably a waste of money. Use single sheets identically formatted to display product. That way, you can add product by simply adding a new catalog sheet instead of going to the expense of printing an entire new catalog. When you've generated enough revenue over a period of time to confirm that your product offering will sell consistently, then is the time to consider a more structured catalog format.

Take a quick look at the Catalogue Page in the Addendum section of this book. Notice there is no pricing on the promo sheet. Some retailers actually hang promo sheets on the wall in the stores for promotion and prefer them not to show a price. And, if you change your pricing, it's much easier to just update the order form.

The sales package sent to retailers should the promo sheet, two order forms, and if possible a sample of your product. Enclose two business cards.

The following cover is structured for selling greeting cards, but is easily adapted for presenting posters, puzzles, tee-shirts or whatever your particular product may be:

> *Dear _____ :*
> *I'd like to introduce my line of Fine Art Greeting Cards.*
> *I've enclosed several sample cards and a promotional piece for your review. Additionally, there are more than a hundred images available at my website and I invite you to visit the site at www.douglasready.com.*
> *The suggested retail price per card is $2.50.*
> *I'm confident your customers will find the cards appealing. I appreciate your consideration of my work and I look forward to speaking with you.*

You can use essentially the same letter for contacting potential Distributors, but with a few minor changes:

> *Dear _____ :*
> *I'd like to introduce my line of Fine Art Greeting Cards.*
> *I've enclosed several sample cards and a promotional piece for your review. Additionally, there are more than a hundred images available at my website and I invite you to visit the site at www.douglasready.com.*
> *The suggested retail price per card is $2.50.*
> *I'm currently looking to form a relationship with a Distributor in your area. I'm confident your customers will find the cards appealing.*
> *I appreciate your consideration of my work and I look forward to speaking with you."*

The letters are simple and direct. If the imagery on your product fails to interest the prospect, nothing you can say in a cover letter is going to make one bit of difference.

Include a complete order form, one that also lists the images that are on the website, but not on the promo sheet. The promo sheet should have a printed invitation to visit the website for additional images. If the size of your product doesn't prohibit it, enclose a sample for retailers. Even if size makes the prospect somewhat unwieldy, always enclose a product sample when contacting distributors.

Don't send promo packages to stores or distributing firms, send them to people. Call the store or the distributing firm and ask for a name. Packages delivered without a specific addressee are often relegated to the junk mail pile and are sometimes disposed of without ever being opened. At this point, you don't need to speak to the person, you just need to know who to direct the package to so you know who to follow up with.

Operate on the assumption that a package dropped into the mail without a telephone follow-up call is a waste of postage.

Telephone the prospect seven to ten days after you've mailed the package. Make certain the package has arrived and ask if there's been a chance to look over the material. Answer any questions--everybody has questions. Verbally invite the prospect to visit your website catalog.

And always ask if the prospect is ready to place an order every time you talk with them. The most you get in business is what your ask for.

### The Website as a Sales & Marketing Tool

Your website is one of the most effective--and inexpensive--sales and marketing tools at your disposal. It gives you the opportunity to put your product catalog in front of everyone in the world that has access to a computer, and all without print cost.

Your website should certainly contain all the images you have available. As mentioned earlier, the imagery should be easy to access without a lot of splashy animation involved in the web page setup to aggravate those potential customers who find their way to your site. The concentration span of the modern consumer is extremely short--this isn't meant as an insult, but rather an observational statement of fact--and if your visitor has to wait longer than a few seconds for your page to load, chances are that he won't.

Your URL should be listed on every piece of business paraphernalia associated with your business: business cards, promotional pieces, catalog pages, invoices, packing slips, and definitely on your letterhead. The URL should also be printed on each and every one of your products. It doesn't need to be an overt invitation to visit your site, just print the URL below your company name along with a copyright notice.

If you are selling directly to consumers on the site, consumers should be directed to their own section. If you're selling wholesale on the site, it's a good idea to have a separate wholesale section. Post a link on the first page of your site that will take the wholesaler to where he needs to be.

A printable order forms is a must, even if you're set up for online ordering. Give your customers the option of ordering in whatever manner is comfortable for them.

Clearly state minimum order requirements. Tell your customers approximately how long they'll have to wait for merchandise, retail or wholesale, and make certain the orders go out in a timely fashion.

If you're interested in talking with distributing firms, convey that information on a separate and distinct page from the other pages.

## Direct to Consumer

If your published designs are guaranteed to appeal to a small market--sometimes called a "niche" market--selling directly to the consumer may be your most effective method of generating income.

You'll focus on internet sales and probably spend a good bit of your promotion and selling time in direct contact situations, i.e., street and craft fairs.

The key to success in niche marketing is to build a loyal fan base of customers who will return time and time again to add to their collection of your product. It's important to maintain a contact list of those people you encounter with an interest in your product and to keep them updated regularly of new additions to your product line.

## Rattling the Retailer

The real key to putting your product into the stores is personal contact, preferably face-to-face, but distance sometimes necessitates the use of the telephone. Nobody orders what they don't like, of course, but often what they do like gets lost in the shuffle. Personal contact helps assure that the retailer will remember--and purchase--those products with a potential for his own profitability.

Establishing solid working relationships with a network of Distributors is the most effective method of putting your product into the stores.

Retailers generally pay fifty percent of the retail price to purchase cards from the manufacturer. To qualify for this wholesale price, you'll want to establish a minimum purchase amount. You are most certainly free to determine at what dollar point selling at a substantial discount is worth your while, but the important thing is consistency and fairness: establish a wholesale minimum and stick to it so that your customers know what to expect.

Shipping is one of those negotiable issues, but most art publishing companies do charge for shipping. It's become increasingly convenient for the retailer to supply the vendor with a UPS number to be used for product delivered to his store. UPS bills the retailer directly for shipping, so no shipping charge is noted on your product invoice.

Occasionally, retailers will suggest you place your product with them on consignment. Don't be fooled: they aren't offering to do you a favor.

You want to find the retailer who believes in your product enough, that is believes your product actually has a decent chance to sell to his customer base, to make a financial investment in your product and in your company. You aren't looking for some storekeeper who's looking to fill in his empty racks at your expense. The retailer who isn't willing to invest in your product probably isn't willing to prominently display it, isn't willing to rotate your product so that it's seen to best advantage and definitely isn't willing to reorder--I mean order--product to refill his coffers.

Horror stories abound. With no financial investment in product, the retailer has no obligation to even put your product in the display rack. Damaged merchandise that the retailer won't assume responsibility for costs you money in product, money in printing and distribution, and money in time that could have been spent pursuing a real customer.

The initial investment to stock your product in a retail store is minimal. The effort required to acquire your cards at no cost is less than minimal.

### Chains, Chains, Chains

Chain stores offer some interesting challenges to the budding art publishing entrepreneur, but offer extraordinary opportunity as well.

The biggest advantage to marketing your product to a

chain is the potential to place your product in ten, twenty, fifty or even a hundred or more stores in one fell swoop. Chain stores are pursued in exactly the same manner you pursue the independent retailer, but the sample package is sent to the headquarters location and directed to the corporate buyer responsible for purchasing your particular variety of published product. Any branch location of a chain store will direct you to the headquarters location and a quick telephone call will identify the proper contact there.

It's important to make certain your production issues are locked in before contacting a potential client who has the capability of placing an order for several thousand items. Failure to deliver a substantial order in a timely manner is pretty much guaranteed to prevent any future order from that organization.

Shipping can also be a concern when dealing with the chain store customer. Some organizations prefer that product is delivered to a headquartered warehouse for distribution to the stores, others require that product is delivered to each individual retail location. Without proper planning, shipping can become a logistical nightmare.

In some instances, chain stores will request that you add a bar code to the back of your product for purposes of inventory control. In most cases, the chain store will provide their bar code to you if you request that they do so.

The most efficient way to quickly grow your business is to place your product in several chains. Just make sure you're prepared to adequately deal with the drastic increase in volume.

### Dealing with Distributors

Without a doubt, the most important relationship you can build in the art publishing business is with a distributor.

Art publishing is a people business and the people involved in the business prefer to deal with people. As a creator and manufacturer you can certainly call on retailers yourself, assuming your sales skills are up to the task, but even assuming you're the best salesman to come down the pike since P.T. Barnum, simple distance will prevent you from contacting enough potential customers to achieve the kind of continuing financial success you'd like to realize from your efforts.

Wholesale Representatives, sometimes referred to as Distributors, serve as selling agents for manufacturers and publishers. Wholesale Representatives agree to carry those products they believe they can sell and make money on.

They sell your product to retailers at a wholesale price and a paid on commission based on the number of dollars generated in sales for your company. The percentages vary from product to product, but a good general rule is that the wholesaler will expect a 15-20% commission on sales. This commission is separate and has no effect on the wholesale price paid by the retailer, so if you're inclined to explore publishing greeting cards or posters you'll need to factor a wholesaler's commission into your retail price to insure a profit.

You'll be expected to provide a complete sample kit of your product to the Wholesaler--if you are publishing greeting cards, for example, you'll provide product catalogs, order forms and samples of the cards, as well. Legitimate Wholesale Representatives pay all of their other expenses, so if you get a bill for lunches and gasoline immediately sever the relationship.

Most wholesalers are specialists. Sometimes that specialization is based on a particular kind of product, sometimes on the particular kind of customer the wholesaler is familiar with. It isn't unusual for a greeting card wholesaler to also handle certain types of gift items or photo albums or even candles, because the type of retailer he calls on is likely to carry all of these items.

Wholesale Representatives are most easily identified by consulting Trade Directory publications. A Google search under the proper heading--"poster wholesalers or distributors"--will turn up a healthy prospect list.

I'm not suggesting you abandon calling on customers yourself or mailing your promotional retail packages. In many cases an effective promotional package followed up with a friendly phone call will result in product placement, but I'm willing to bet that if you accurately track your selling efforts--something you should be doing as a matter of course--you'll find that your percentage of acquired customers is much higher among those retailers you've talked to in person than among those you've contacted by mail.

Distributors generally work a specific geographic area. The Rep will probably want exclusivity for your line within that geographic area.

When trying to recruit distributors, send them product samples, a product catalog and a letter of introduction. Include a price list and ask if they'd be interested in carrying your line. The Spoors Rep Directory is a good reference volume to identify distributors and the Greeting Card Association will also sell you a list of distributors.

There's also a list of distributors in the Addendum to this handbook, as well as some no-cost suggestions for identifying Reps.

Sales representation is a difficult issue and it's the main reason so many small art publishing companies don't last through their first year in operation. Finding reliable, professional sales representatives to take on your line has to be a priority from the moment you hang up your company sign. Distributors are an essential tool for your company's growth. Retailers overwhelmingly prefer dealing face-to-face with a sales person to mail order. A reliable sales representative will have on-going relationships with dozens of retailers.

A big part of the frustration of this business is the distributor who agrees to take your line and then produces no sales at all. If your distributors aren't selling within the first three months of taking on your line, talk to them, find out why and if necessary take the steps to replace that distributor with one who will provide results.

Concentrate first on finding distributors in all the big metropolitan areas: New York, Boston, Los Angeles, Chicago, Dallas, Atlanta, Seattle, Denver--then, expand your distributor network to those areas that are less densely populated.

Different distributors will want different things from you. Some will want just a complete product catalog. Some will want samples of each and every product you produce. It's to your benefit to provide your distributor with exactly what he says he needs to do a good job for you.

Some distributors will ask you to sign a contract, but most won't. That said, it's a good idea to have some sort of written agreement specifying commission percentages--the industry average is 15-20% of dollars generated in product sold-- and when and how those commissions are paid. Terms are always negotiable. Generally, you'll either pay your distributor at the end of the month in which the order comes in, the end of the month in which the order is shipped and invoiced, or the end of the month in which the retailer pays you. Put it in writing, even if only in letter form, something to the effect "...this is to confirm our conversation regarding your company representing my line." It's important to know that your understanding of the financial partnership are the same as the distributor's. Make sure to keep a copy for your records.

NEVER sign an agreement with a distributor that obligates you to particular distributor representation for longer than three months. If the distributor isn't producing, you'll want to find another. If the distributor, for whatever reason, simply decides he doesn't want to show your product, he can literally stop you from selling in his geographic area if you've signed a contract granting him exclusive representation for a specified period of time.

Look for a distributor that has experience with small publishers. It's important that the distributor actually like your work because it's virtually impossible to sell a product one doesn't care for. And, it's especially easy for your product to get lost in the bottom of his sample case if he lacks a fondness for your work.

### International Sales

International Sales are best left to those distributing firms that have experience in this area or foreign distributing firms that have experience importing products into their own countries. The procedure for contact is exactly the same, but a variety of additional factors, such as tariffs and international shipping, need to be considered. It's probably best to first concentrate on the domestic market and grow into the international market when the dollars you're generating justify the expansion.

### Marketing, Marketing, Marketing

From a strictly business perspective, the most important thing you can do each and every day is to put your product in front of a new prospect and ask him to buy it. Of course, you must first identify a prospect. This can be tricky, but here are several techniques you might find helpful.

A good many of us shirk away from the idea of direct selling, that is, physically carrying your product into a retail store, introducing yourself to the store owner or manager, presenting your line and then asking to buy. It can be intimidating, but if you'll internalize the notion that you're dealing with a product, not the expression of your creative urges, and listen carefully to the responses you get you'll learn much more much more quickly about placing your product than you'll ever learn from any handbook.

The simple truth is, you need to carry your product into a couple of stores.  Even if your plans call for a marketing blitz directed solely at distributors and you never plan to actually call on retailers as part of your marketing strategy, it's extremely helpful to have retailer feedback tucked away for your conversation with a potential sales rep.  If you talk to one retailer and you don't like his response, forget it and move onto the next one.  On the other hand, if you talk to half-a dozen of them and they all suggest the same problem, you might want to give the matter some thought before spending all that money mailing packages to distributors.

**Expanding Your Product Line**
The imagery you produce is well on its way to penetrating the market.  It's important to continue promoting, marketing and selling your line, but it's also important to fully utilize your images to maximize your income.

In some cases, expanding your product line to include different kinds of product is a prudent move.  If your line of greeting cards have proven successful, consider a move into poster and production or possibly bookmarks or note cards, especially if some of your existing customers would be interested in carrying your imagery in additional formats. Expanding into these kinds of product areas makes logistical since because you've already done the necessary production research to launch your greeting card line and a lot of that legwork will readily transfer to your new offering.  Of course you'll need to blend the new products into your promotional and sales efforts and proceed accordingly.

You can, of course, secure reproduction of your imagery on any number of consumer products--mugs, clothing, and lunchboxes--by simply picking up the telephone and hiring a production company to do the work.  This is sometimes known as "private label" production--another company makes the product, but your label is on it--and depending on the particular products involved the necessary cash investment can be substantial. And, you've got to stockpile a large number of different items so that they're readily available should any of your customers decide to order them.

A number of companies are structured to allow the artist to reproduce his image on a wide variety of products without the necessity of investing in production. Companies like Cafe Press (www.cafepress.com) will produce imagery ordered in increments as small as a single unit when ordered directly by the consumer from their web site, but their operational apparatus presents limitations. There are a limited number of products available for personalization and since product is purchased in single units as the orders come in the profit margin for the artist usually leaves a great deal to be desired. A low profit margin is the trade-off for limited investment, but product promotion is largely left to the artist and often the investment return on time spent simply doesn't generate enough volume to make the effort worthwhile.

**Selling the Original Art**

I'm always amazed at the number of artists producing work primarily designed for reproduction who have stacks of the original art tucked into drawers and closets. The most personally undemanding method of increasing your product offering is to make your original artwork available for purchase.

Often, your retail clients will be delighted to hang one or two of your originals on their wall in exchange for a commission on the sale. In fact, the original art on the wall will often direct customers to the reproduced greeting cards in the retailer's racks, resulting in more sales.

Simply posting the art on your web site with a price tag is sometimes all it takes. Originals may be Gallery Quality work, and that avenue should be explored if appropriate.

Originals can be auctioned on EBAY, sold at Street Fairs, donated to Charities...

The point is that original art does nothing to benefit the artist if it's left hiding in a bureau. If there are particular pieces you want to retain for your portfolio or hang on your own wall, then by all means do so, but take whatever steps necessary to liquidate those pieces you're willing to let go.

At the very least, use the originals as promotional gambits in your marketing efforts.

### Production & Promotion Issues

Paper, printing, envelopes, storing, shipping, discounts, turnaround time, backorders, web-building, catalogs, sample kits, promotional expenses...

When you begin to break the art publishing business down into its components, it can seem a little overwhelming, especially when you realize that, at least in the beginning, you're the one who is responsible for each and every one of them.

Simple is better. This should be obvious, but I am constantly amazed at how complicated people are inclined to make things. Have you ever listened to a sales pitch for cellular phone service? Please, just tell me how much a minute...

As a manufacturing entrepreneur, you'll not only be a vendor you'll be doing business with vendors. These are the folks who supply your paper and envelopes and pencils and printing and shipping services. It is much simpler to deal with local vendors than to deal with long-distance vendors.

If there's a problem with a print job, it's much easier-- and quicker--to drive twenty minutes across town and talk to your printer than it is to package your order, return it half-way across country and try to explain via telephone, email or fax just exactly why what you got wasn't what you asked for.

The same goes for product. Unless you're prepared to buy in large enough quantities to negate shipping charges, the amount of money you save buying paper online may not be enough to justify the delay in getting your hands on your stock.

Yes, there are certainly instances where working with a local supplier simply isn't practical, but it is recommended that you investigate local suppliers and do a comprehensive cost comparison before limiting yourself to a supplier you don't have physical access to.

If you decide to use long-distance suppliers, it's a good idea to have a local supplier lined up as a backup.

Printing is probably the biggest production concern for the self-publishing artist. It probably isn't practical to personally print your final product, but it may be cost-effective, at least in the beginning stages of your publishing operation, to print your own promotional material.

There are a number of more than adequate home printers available for well under $100. The three primary considerations are quality, speed and the number of printed sheets to cartridge refill. Inkjet printers have finally reached a point where the results compare favorable with the more expensive LaserJet printers, and they are usually less expensive to operate.

Producing sample packages must be an ongoing concern. Your chances of selling are directly proportionate to the number of people who have seen your product.

In the beginning, you should call on a minimum of five retailers in person each week. Leave a sample package, even there is no decision to carry your cards. You'll learn a great many things about the art publishing business, you'll learn a great many things about why people buy art reproductions in whatever form you're producing and why they don't, and you'll probably even learn a few things you can do to improve your chances of placing your product into a greater number of stores. Even if your marketing plan calls for a blitz on distributors and you have no inclination to call on individual retail stores long-term, the experience you'll gain actually calling on retailers for even three or four weeks will prove invaluable.

At a minimum, your promotional efforts should include ten sales packages mailed to retailers each and every week. That means you'll schedule ten follow-up sales calls for the following week.

At a minimum, your promotional efforts should include five sales packages mailed to distributors each and every week. That means you'll schedule an additional five follow-up sales calls for the following week.

You should contact retailers who become customers once a month to introduce new product and solicit new orders.

If you've done the math, you understand that you're going to be very busy. The activity compounds when orders begin to come in, but it's important to maintain the promotion schedule. Your focus will shift as time goes by, depending on the avenues you develop for most effectively selling your product, but your best bet for growth is always going to be promotion.

Your promotional efforts should be carefully coordinate to make the best use of both time and cost. Carefully consider your options and commit only to those promotional efforts you recognize as having a real potential to increase sales.

Still, you need to make the time to create new product. Chances are that creating the product was what you found so enchanting in the first place. Creation not only recharges you, it presents new product to market which is paramount if your company is to thrive in a competitive market.

Finding suppliers for virtually any production component or promotional tool is as easy as opening the Yellow Pages or visiting Google online at www.google.com. The hard part is determining which supplier is appropriate for your immediate situation, and the only way to do that is to sift through a number of them before the need occurs.

## Productivity & Tracking Systems

### Inspect What You Expect

An old proverb suggests that in order to figure out where one is going, he must first determine where he is.

Tracking accomplishment is an absolute necessity to achieve success in any business, but especially in the art business. Notice I said tracking accomplishment, not tracking activity.

Splitting one's focus between producing and promoting can quickly become a confusing prospect. Therefore, keeping a written log of what needs to be done--in both areas--when it needs to be done and that in fact it was done is of primary importance.

### Checklists

There are any number of computer software programs that allow the user to list activities, goals, contacts and schedules--in fact, there is probably some sort of Scheduling Program build into the software that came on your computer. Most of these programs will do an adequate job of keeping you on the straight and narrow, assuming you're willing to take the time and put the information into the system.

You may find, however, that a basis Excel spreadsheet is the most effective method of keeping track of both your creative production activities and your promotional activities. Blocks and columns are easily adapted to your own specific tracking requirements and you'll have the added bonus of being able to block in and total expenses and sales figures from your efforts on the same sheet.

Whatever method you decide to set-up, take fifteen minutes every day and update to keep yourself on track.

### Systems & Tactical Response

**Licenses, Fees & Sales Tax**

Every state or province and virtually every locale requires a license to operate a business. Specific requirements and statutes vary from place to place, but what it all boils down to is that the municipality in which you live is going to charge you for the privilege of conducting business inside its borders.

Depending on the scope of your business operation, there are other fees you might need to concern yourself with. If you're selling retail, you may need to collect sales tax. If you're just selling wholesale, you probably won't need to worry about it, but--again, depending on where you're located--you might still be liable for filing that particular tax paperwork every year to inform them you didn't collect any sales tax monies.

Every state and municipality has an office dedicated to helping you understand just exactly what your obligations and responsibilities are. They've also got an office dedicated to rounding up those folks who don't make the effort.

The Internal Revenue Service offers a free seminar to those people who are considering forming a small business. It deals with a number of issues that probably wouldn't occur to anyone who has never had to file a Federal Tax Return that included self-generated income.

Make sure you contact your local tax office, your state tax office and the IRS before you actually begin presenting your product for sale. Believe it or not, they really are there to help, and they actually want you to be successful. Very successful. The more successful you are, the more taxes they're allowed to collect.

**Using the Business License to Best Advantage**

Many of us tend to view a Business License solely as a

legal obligation we must pay. Used properly, possessing a license can actually increase your profitability.

Generally speaking, supplies bought for use in production of products that will be presented for sale are non-taxable, even when bought at the retail level. You'll have to show your license and the store will probably have you sign a Reseller Statement certifying your purchase is just that, but in Washington State the sales tax is right at 10%--saving $10 for every $100 I spend on supplies makes it worthwhile to take a moment and fill out the paperwork. And, a great many retailers will offer a professional discount if they've seen your license.

### Keeping Those Records Up To Date

The fledgling small business person usually gets into trouble because he or she failed to document those things that directly influence the bottom line. Sometimes, that trouble is delivered via a third party, i.e., a bill collector or a tax collector, and sometimes trouble shows up all by its lonesome because somebody failed to note that a huge chain store order absolutely had to be shipped no later than ten days ago and you've got no reasonable explanation for the buyer on the phone who took a chance on your line and now all your Valentine's Cards aren't going to arrive in 40 stores until the day before the holiday...

The art publishing business requires four things:

1. **You need to design and manufacture product.**
2. **You need to sell product.**
3. **You need to ship product.**
4. **You need to get paid for product.**

Lots of little things happen between each step, and all of it needs to be documented. It's important to know exactly where you are at any point in the game, even if you're the only one keeping score. Someday, you won't be the only one at the tally board and you'll need those systems you've become comfortable with to help you work both as a vendor and with vendors supplying you.

It isn't necessary to invest in expensive record-keeping software. You can set up a simple income/outgo dollar sheet in Excel, and it's a pretty good idea to set up a Tracking Sheet as well, one that will tell you when an order was placed, who placed it, how much the order was for, whatever special instructions might be attached to the order, where it being shipped to, and when it was shipped. For good luck, add a column to list when it was paid for.

### Accounts Payable & Accounts Receivable

First, let's define some basic accounting terms in very plain English:

> *Invoice:* This is the bill you send to the customer who's made a purchase. It tells him what was ordered, what was sent and how much money he owes you. You should assign each invoice a number for tracking purposes.

> *Purchase Order:* This is a request from a customer for merchandise. Many companies will issue a "purchase order" which is in effect a permission slip to purchase. Always note the number on the Purchase Order--sometimes called the "P.O. Number"--on the invoice you send to the customer.

> *Receipt:* This is the verification that something has been either purchased or delivered. If you're delivering orders yourself, make certain someone at the store signs a statement that an order has been delivered and appears to have been delivered in good condition. This is your

proof that they've got the merchandise and now need to pay you. If you're mailing the merchandise or using a delivery service, always request a receipt of delivery-- someone will sign for the package and you'll get a confirmation of delivery. It's a good idea to note the packing slip number on any receipt paperwork in case there's a need to track it.

*Packing Slip:* This is the inventory list that goes inside the package delivered to the customer. It lists what merchandise is inside the box and how many of each piece. This is the list the customer uses to make certain that what was ordered is actually what was delivered. You should assign each packing slip a number that correlates with the invoice for the order. In the event of a problem, tracking becomes much easier.

Keep copies of every Invoice, Purchase Order, Receipt and Packing Slip. You'll need the for tracking purposes and you'll need them for tax purposes.

Retailers will generally purchase your product for a wholesale price that is equal to 50% of the retail price. In order to qualify for the wholesale price, the retailer should be required to purchase a minimum wholesale amount. Standards vary. You'll want to set a minimum that insures a reasonable profit, even at the wholesale rate, but at the same time isn't so elevated that your potential retail customer runs away in shock.

Retailers who do not enclose full payment with their order require billing. It is normal procedure to enclose an invoice with the packing slip. That said, use your own judgment. If your customer orders using his own purchase order, read the instructions thoroughly. Some chain stores will want the product sent to each individual store, and individual invoices sent to the headquarter location.

Independent retailers ordering by mail or via the internet for the first time should probably be required to include payment for the full amount of the purchase. There are always exceptions, but you'll save yourself a good many sleepless nights if you try to get that first order paid for when it is placed. Orders placed when you visit a retail store, even if it's a first visit, are generally expected to be invoiced at the time of delivery.

Of course, it is preferred all orders are accompanied by full payment, but if the store prefers to be billed, most art publishers generally honor that request starting with the second order. Most retailers will pay an invoice "Net 30", but what that really means is the invoice will sit on somebody's desk until the end of the month and be processed sometime within the 30 days after that. The average is 45-60 days before receiving payment. New orders should never be processed until previous orders have been paid for.

It's not generally a good idea to accept orders over the telephone. Refer the buyer to your website or offer to send them an order form. The order form details a complete product listing and your company contact information, but most importantly, it has a signature box authorizing the order and agreeing to pay for it. That little detail is paramount if it becomes necessary to pursue a retailer for collection.

If "Net 30" doesn't happen in "Net 45-60" it's entirely appropriate to call the Accounting Department, ask for Accounts Payable and talk to someone who can determine the status of your invoice. The accounting department will ask you for the invoice number. Enter whatever comment you receive, as well as the name of the person you spoke with and the date, on your Tracking Sheet. Sadly, there are those instances where one telephone call doesn't resolve the matter.

Distributors will generally sell directly to the retailer and forward the order to you. Distributors will generally expect a 20% commission on the dollar volume they've produced, that means that if a retail store places a $100 wholesale order through your Distributor, you bill the retailer for a hundred bucks and you owe the Distributor $20. You will bill the retail store and the Distributor will bill you, or at the very least consider the order he forwarded to you his invoice. Distributors are generally paid by the greeting card manufacturer in one of three ways:

**1. Commission is paid at the end of the month the order came in.**

**2. Commission is paid at the end of the month the order is shipped.**

**3. Commission is paid at the end of the month the retailer pays the manufacturer.**

It's an absolute necessity to have a written agreement in place with your Distributor outlining financial policy, even if that agreement is a just a letter confirming a "20% commission that will be paid at the end of the month the manufacturer payment from the retailer for the full invoice amount."

If there's a potential for a problem, you want to know well before it becomes one.

**The Tax Man Cometh**
Possession of a business license announces your serious intent to tax authorities. You're now responsible for state and federal income taxes, any local income taxes, sales taxes that must be collected on retail sales and forwarded to the state, and any additional fees for services that might not readily be apparent.

On a more positive note, many of the costs of operating

a business are tax deductible, meaning those costs are deducted from your income and you are only taxed on the difference between the two.

In addition to expenses for supplies and postage, if you're working out of your home a portion of your rent or mortgage and your utilities is probably now tax deductible as a business expense. Should you decide to incorporate, things like Health Insurance and other company-paid benefits may be deductible.

Requirements vary from state to state, as well as from circumstance to circumstance, , so it's best to talk with a tax professional. The idea is to pay every single cent of the taxes you owe, but not a penny more, and a tax professional is in a much better position to insure that you take advantage of every deduction.

Incidentally, the tax professional's fee is also deductible.

### The Art of Success

The only constant is change.

In the course of pursuing a profitable career as an art publisher, your product will evolve into something that originally would never have occurred to you, and your promotional efforts will diversify and result in opportunities you might never have considered.

The information presented in this seminar should be viewed as a place to begin, not as a one-way roadmap to your eventual destination. Notice the signs along the way and carefully select those turns which might be to your benefit.

So, you've created your product, you've got a pretty good idea of how you're going to produce it, and you've got a proven mechanism for marketing it.

I wish you the very best of luck.

## Appendix

What follows are resources most every working artist will have a need for at one time or another. Items such as Invoices or Bills of Sale should of course be printed on the Artist's Letterhead.

### Artists & Illustrator's Directories

*Graphic Artist's Guild Directory of Illustration*
http://www.directoryofillustration
Extensive online portfolio gallery of professional illustrators.

*The Workbook (Illustrators)*
http://www.workbook.com/assignment/illustrators/
Extensive online portfolio gallery of professional illustrators.

*I Spot*
http://www.theispot.com/
Extensive online portfolio gallery of illustrators.

*Spectrum: The Best in Contemporary Fantastic Art*
http://www.spectrumfantasticart.com/
Spectrum features a variety of Fantasy, Science Fiction and Comic Book Art. Released annually, the volume is sold as an oversized trade paperback in book stores.

**Bill of Sale for Original Art**

Date:_____

Title:

_____

_____

Sold
to:_____

_____

      Address:

_____

–

_____

–

      Telephone:                  _____Email:

_____

                 Price:          $_____

                 Shipping:     $_____

                 Total:          $_____

Unless otherwise specifically indicated, all works herein are originals executed by the artist and are certified to be free from defects due to faulty craftsmanship or faulty materials for a period of twelve months from the date of sale. If flaws should appear during this period and be due to such causes, said works shall be subject to repair or replacement at the option of the seller. Buyer is cautioned, however, that the seller cannot be responsible for fading, cracking, and other damage to the work caused by improvident exposure to sunlight and weather.

All shipments are fully insured by the shipper against damage or loss. If works are not received in good condition, please notify the seller within ten days of receipt. All shipments will be transferred via freight collect unless prepaid by the buyer. Crating methods and charges are per art object freight company standard procedures and rates.

The original works described herein are copyrighted by the artist. The sale of such copyrighted work does not include the sale of rights to reproduction in any form unless specifically granted in writing by the artist.

_____

                                                     Artist

**Print Certificate of Authenticity**

Date:_____

Title:

_____

_____

This is to certify that the print entitled **(Name of Print)** is an original by **(Name of Artist)**.

Number of authorized signed prints in the Edition: _____

Number of individual print: _____

The original works described herein are copyrighted by the artist. The sale of such copyrighted work does not include the sale of rights to reproduction in any form unless specifically granted in writing by the artist.

_____                Artist


_____                Date

## Sample Gallery Contract

Finding a reputable gallery that wants to represent you and your work is at best a daunting task. More daunting is wading through the contract the gallery will hopefully present to you.

I say hopefully because many artists and dealers seem to want to base their business relationship on a handshake and word, but unless your spouse or your mother runs the gallery that represents you, make sure you get all agreements in writing.

Contracts are a good thing for an artist to have. A well-written contract protects you from any misunderstandings--or misrepresentations--that arise pertaining to the handling of your work. If an artist does not have a written contract with a gallery, then the gallery has all the power to decide how it will handle the artist's creations.

A contract outlines specific guidelines and criteria to meet the needs of both the artist and the gallery or dealer. These guidelines include pricing of work, commissions received on work sold, when and how the artist will be paid, how many pieces a gallery exhibits, how long and how often the work is shown, and in general, the responsibilities of both the artist and the gallery to each other.

Most galleries will offer a formal contract. Before signing it, *make sure you read everything in it* and ask questions if anything seems confusing or doesn't apply to you. If there are changes you want made in the contract, suggest these to the gallery. The best tool you and the gallery have in negotiating a contract is clear communication. Many galleries are willing to come to terms and make compromises with individual artists to suit their varied specific needs.

Some galleries may not have a standard contract. You can have a contract specially drawn up to meet both your needs.

If a gallery refuses to sign a contract with you, reconsider allowing that gallery to represent your work. When you turn over work to a gallery without anything in writing and something goes wrong, you're pretty much left holding the bag.

A gallery contract should spell out an inventory list with complete, accurate titles or descriptions of the work the gallery is receiving along with the retail prices of each piece of work the gallery will be holding.

The amount of the commission to be paid must be in the contract. The gallery commission may range up to 50% , and many galleries take their commission out of your original asking price. For example, if you price a work at $1000 and the gallery's commission is 50%, when the work is sold, the gallery receives $500 and you receive $500. Some galleries add their commission to the original price, thus increasing the selling price, i.e., if you've priced a painting at $1000, the gallery receives a 50% commission if the piece is sold, so $500 is added to your asking price and the work sells in the gallery for $1500.

You receive your original $1000 asking price and the gallery receives $500.

Before pricing your work, make sure to find out how the commission is added. You want to keep your prices as consistent as possible wherever you choose to show your work. If you're serious about gallery representation, picking up a reputation of undercutting galleries' prices will put you soundly out of the game.

Within the contract, it will be mentioned how long the gallery will keep the work on display. Some galleries schedule solo exhibitions for artists, others keep work on consignment for group shows. Most will operate with a combination of the two. Galleries that take pieces on consignment are often flexible about how long they will keep work--often three to six months, and even longer if the gallery has been successful in selling some of the work.

Another concern is cost of delivering and removing work from the gallery. If you haven't developed a solid track record of generating large gallery sales, the most likely you'll be in charge of getting your work to the gallery and getting it out when the exhibition is done.

Galleries that conduct solo exhibitions for artists may hold receptions or leave it up to the artist to be responsible for the reception. Specific responsibility for receptions need to be spelled out in the contract: publicity, printing and mailing cost of invitations, refreshments--get it all in writing. The last thing you want is to walk in opening night to an unattended opening.

The contract should clearly state when the gallery pays the artist after a work is sold. Standard practice is to pay the artist at the beginning of the following month. Along with a check, the artist should receive a *Bill of Sale* that lists the date the work was purchased, the title/description of the piece, the retail price, the gallery commission, the artist's commission, and the signature of the person who sold the work. Try to require the gallery to list the name of the client who purchased the work-- that information is invaluable to the artist.

Some galleries will keep works on consignment beyond the average 6 months but under the condition that the works will be discounted in price. Use your own discretion here, but in any event make certain that if the gallery you're dealing with participates in discount pricing that your contract spells out just which one of you will absorb the loss.

One factor to consider is the exclusiveness of the gallery towards your work. The gallery may want you to exhibit only at their location and no other gallery locally. Make certain it is clearly written in the contract if the gallery has limitations on where you can exhibit. Often galleries will encourage artists to sell work from their studios, especially if the artist had clientele prior to representation at the gallery, assuming the artist is willing to forward a percentage of those sales to the gallery (generally a smaller percentage than if the piece sold had actually been purchased from the gallery).

The Sample Contract below is presented as an example. It doesn't pretend to cover all aspects of the Artist's concerns. Ideally, every gallery contract should be an individualized document addressing the particular circumstance faced at every showing. This Sample is presented for clarification purposes and as a guide for constructing your own contract should the need arise.

Never sign a gallery contract--or any contract, for that matter--that you haven't read and understand completely. When in doubt, talk to an attorney who specialized in the Visual Arts. It's cheaper in the long run.

**Sample Gallery Contract**

It is hereby agreed between _____(the Artist) and _____ (the Dealer)  that the dealer shall exhibit the artist's work at the dealer's premises under the following conditions:

> 1. The works hereby consigned for exhibition and sale by the dealer as agent for the artist are enumerated, described, and priced at retail on the attached list. Such works are warranted by the artist: to be his/her own original creations, and to be the unencumbered property of the artist. They shall remain the property of the artist unless and until they are purchased by collectors or by the dealer.
>
> 2. The works here listed shall be exhibited by the dealer from _____ (date) to and including _____ (date). These works shall constitute a **(solo/part of a group)** exhibition. Such exhibitions

shall be held approximately every _____ months.

3. Approximately _____ works on the attached list shall be hung during the exhibition period. The reminder shall be available for inspection by prospective purchasers. After the exhibition period. the artist's consigned works may be retained by the dealer for sale for a term of _____ months. At the end of that period, they may be individually removed by the artist providing five days prior written notice has been given. Other works may be supplied as additions or replacements for works sold or removed from time to time by mutual written agreement of artist and dealer. The term for retention of works may be thereafter extended annually by mutual written agreement.

4. The artist will assist the dealer by: **(select appropriate responsibilities)**
    A.  Crating and shipping works to the dealer
    B.  Framing the works for exhibition
    C.  Furnishing advice, cooperation, and assistance in advertising and publicizing the artist's work
    D.  Furnishing data regarding prospective and existing collectors.

5. The dealer will pay the artist _____ % of the retail sales price on any works sold. Notice of all sales, including the name and address of purchaser will be given to the artist at the conclusion of each month and payment of all monies due shall be made not more than thirty days after the receipt of payment by the dealer.

The dealer assumes full risk of non-payment by the purchaser. However, if a work is returned in good condition by a client for credit, the dealer will make appropriate pro rata adjustments in future payments to the artist.

6. During the term of this agreement or any extension thereof and during the shipment to the artist of works from the dealer, the dealer shall cause all of the artist's works consigned to the dealer to be insured to the benefit of the artist against any and all loss in an amount equal to the artist's portion of the retail sales price.

7. No unsold works shall be removed from the dealer's premises and no discounts shall be permitted except by specific permission of the artist.

8. The artist shall have the right to inventory all consigned works at reasonable times and to obtain a full accounting for any works not present at the dealer's premises at such time.

9. The artist reserves all rights to the reproduction of works in any manner. This restriction shall be indicated by the dealer in writing on all sales invoices and memoranda. However the artist will not withhold permission for the reproduction of such works for promotional purposes.

10. During the term of this agreement, the dealer will exclusively represent the artist in the following geographical                                                              area:

_____

_____

_____.

However, the artist takes the following exceptions to such exclusive representation: the artist reserves the right to sell works from his/her own studio. In this case, the artist will remit _____ % 01 the proceeds 0f such sales to the dealer.

11. Costs of crating and shipping shall be absorbed by the **Artist / Dealer**.

12. Promotion and advertising costs shall be absorbed by the **Artist / Dealer**.

13. Costs of an exhibition opening in conjunction with the exhibition provided above shall be absorbed by the **Artist / Dealer**.

In the event that a dispute arises under this agreement involving the interpretation of any of the provisions herein which cannot be resolved by discussion between the artist and the dealer, both parties will submit such dispute to an arbitrator appointed by the American Arbitration Association, who shall decide the issue in accordance with the terms of the agreement and the laws of the State of _____. Costs in such cases shall be borne equally by both parties.

_____

_____

Artist

      Date

_____

_____

Dealer

      Date

## Sample Commissioned Art Agreement

1. Agreement

This is an agreement between **(Name)** _____ of **(Company Name)** _____, hereinafter referred to as the Client and **(Artist's Name)** _____, hereinafter referred to as the Artist, for the creation and transfer of the Work. All right and liabilities of either party in the work shall be governed by this agreement.

2. Description of the Work

The work to be created by the artist shall be **(specifications of the work commissioned, including number of images, size and medium)**.

3. Obligations of the Artist and the Client

A. The **(Artist / Client)** shall designate and purchase materials necessary for the creation of the work.

B. The Client shall bear the expense of any transportation or living cost incurred by Artist away from his home or studio, long-distance telephone calls, sales taxes, or customs duties, insofar as such expenses are reasonably incident to or entailed by the Artist's creation, delivery or installation of the work (or supervision thereof).

C. The Artist shall create the Work.

D. The **(Artist / Client)** shall provide for the framing and installation of the work, at the **(Artist / Client)** expense, subject to the Artist's right to supervise any such work.

E.     **(Artist / Client)** shall hire and compensate any additional labor services necessary for the creation and installation of the Work.

F. The **(Artist / Client)** shall obtain insurance on the Work to be in effect until delivery of the completed Work.

4.  Start and Completion dates
    The artist shall undertake the creation of the work on approximately **(Date)** and shall complete the Work by **(Date).**

5.  Fees and Schedule of Payment
    The Client shall pay to the Artist the sum of $_____ in total payment for the work.  This amount shall be paid in equal one-third installments as follows: $_____ upon execution of this agreement; $_____ upon the Client's approval of the Artist's preliminary designs of the Work; and $_____ upon completion and delivery of the completed work.

6.  Cancellation and Cancellation Fee
    The Client shall not unreasonably withhold acceptance of or payment for the Work.  If prior to the Work's completion, the client observes or otherwise becomes aware of nay fault or defect in the work or nonconformance with the design plan, he shall notify the Artist promptly.  However, the client's objection to any feature of the work not specifically indicated by the design plan but attributable to the exercise of the artist's esthetic judgment in the creation of the work on the basis of the design plan shall not justify the Client's withholding acceptance of or payment for the work.

In the event that the Client unreasonably reject the work after having made one or two installment payments, the Artist shall be entitled to keep any monies so paid. In the Event that the Client rejects the Work upon completion and delivery and refuses to pay the final payment installment, the Artist shall be entitled to retain all monies previously paid by the Client and shall also retain full and complete ownership of the Work.

7. Copyright

The Artist shall copyright the work in his own name **(and such rights shall not be affected by the transfer of the work itself / but the artist shall assign all such rights to the client effective with the transfer of the Work itself and the full payment of all monies due the Artist).**

8. Maintenance of the Work

The client shall notify the artist promptly in the event of the need for any maintenance or restoration services so that the artist may have a reasonable opportunity either to perform such work himself or to supervise or consult in its performance. The Artist shall be reasonably compensated by the client for all such maintenance or restoration services. In the absence of any need for restoration or maintenance, the work shall remain free of alteration by the client, who shall take reasonable precautions to protect it against damage or destruction by external forces.

9. Warranty

The Artist warrants that the completed work will be fit and suitable for use and exploitation in the manner for which it is to be created, but this warranty is condition upon the client's compliance with the provisions hereof relation to installation, maintenance and exploitation.

10. Delivery

The Artist shall prepare the work to be ready for delivery to the client on **(Date).** Delivery and physical transfer of the Work shall be accomplished **(by the Artist's notification to the Client that the Work is ready for pick-up at the Artist's studio / by the Artist's causing the work to be sent, insurance and shipping charges prepaid, to the Client).**

11. Title of Ownership

Title of Ownership of the Work shall pass from the Artist to the Client upon the Client's payment of the final installment of the Artist's fee for the Work.

13. Death and Disability

In the event of an incapacitating illness or injury of the Artist and a delay arising therefrom in the execution of the Work, the Artist shall notify the client of such delay and the Client's obligation to make payments shall cease until such time as the Artist notifies the Client he has recovered and is ready to resume. The death of the Artist shall terminate this agreement, and the Artist's estate shall be entitled to retain any payment already made by the Client and to be reimbursed for any payments which the Client would have been obliged to pay the Artist. The Client shall be entitled to claim the Work and any unused materials acquired for its execution, and to have the Work completed by another artist without regard to the original design.

14. Arbitration

         Any dispute hereunder between the parties not involving money claims by either party in excess of \$_____ shall be resolved by resort to arbitration in accordance with the standards and procedures of the American Arbitration Association.

Construction of the agreement shall be governed by the State of _____.

_____

Client                                       Artist

_____

Date                                       Date

### Sample Work for Hire Agreement

This is an agreement between **(Name)** _____of **(Company Name)** _____, hereinafter referred to as the Client and (Artist's Name) _____, hereinafter referred to as the Artist, for the creation and transfer of the Work. All right and liabilities of either party in the work shall be governed by this agreement.

1. Artist will create _____ artworks for **(Name of Project).**

2. Artist shall submit the artworks in finished form no later than **(Date).**

3. Client will pay the artist the sum of $_____ for each artwork, to be paid one-half upon delivery of preliminary design studies and one-half upon delivery of the finished artwork.

4. Any and all artwork created pursuant to this agreement shall be considered a Work For Hire and the Client shall be the sole owner of the original artwork and all rights, including copyright in and to the Work for nay and all purposes.

5. Artist warrants that he is the creator of the Work specified here, the Work has not been published previously, that it does not infringe on any right of copyright or personal rights and rights of privacy of any person or entity and that any necessary permissions have been obtained.

6. Artist agrees he is working as an independent free-

lance contractor and will be responsible for payment of all expense incurred in preparation of the Work.

Construction of the agreement shall be governed by the State of _____.

_____

Client                                                           Artist

_____

Date                                                            Date

**Sample Art Publishing Contract**

This is to confirm that **(Name of Art Publishing Company)** has acquired the right to reproduce a painting entitled **(Name of Painting)** (hereafter referred to as "the Work") created by **(Name of Artist)** upon the following terms and conditions:

1. The Artist hereby grants to **(Name of Art Publishing Company)** the exclusive right throughout the world to publish, manufacture, advertise, distribute and sell color reproductions of the Work.

2. Each reproduction of the Work shall be approximately _____ in size, excluding margins.

3. In consideration thereof, **(Name of Art Publishing Company)** shall pay to the Artist upon execution of this Agreement a non-refundable advance in the amount of $_____ against the royalty hereinafter specified.

4. **(Name of Art Publishing Company)** shall pay to the Artist a royalty of _____% per copy of each reproduction of the Work sold by **(Name of Art Publishing Company)** .

5. **(Name of Art Publishing Company)** may cause the Work to be reproduced by such method and by such entities and means as **(Name of Art Publishing Company)** in its sole discretion may select.

6. **(Name of Art Publishing Company)** shall furnish to the Artist, without charge, six (6) reproductions of the Work and the Artist may purchase additional

reproductions at fifty percent (50%) of the retail price of each reproduction.

7.  The Artist shall deliver the Work to **(Name of Art Publishing Company)** simultaneously with the execution of this Agreement. **(Name of Art Publishing Company)** shall retain the Work and shall proceed to promptly have plates made. The Work shall be returned to the Artist within 90 days of the date of this Agreement. While the Work is in the possession of **(Name of Art Publishing Company)**, the Work shall be fully insured against all risks.

8.  Each reproduction will bear a legend indicating the name of the artist.

9.  The ownership of the copyright of the reproduction shall at all times reside with **(Name of Art Publishing Company)** and the ownership of the copyright of the Work shall at all times reside with the Artist.

10.  The Artist Warrants originality, authorship and ownership of the Work. The Artist has the full power to enter into this Agreement.

11.  The Work has not been heretofore used or published and no right in the Work or reproduction thereof has been assigned, licensed or transferred, and the use or publication of the reproduction by **(Name of Art Publishing Company)** will not infringe upon any copyright, proprietary or other right of any third party. The Artist agrees not to authorize others to use or publish the Work during the term of this Agreement.

12.  This Agreement is to continue in effect for the term

of the copyright on the reproduction.

13. **(Name of Art Publishing Company)** shall keep accurate records with respect to all transactions herein contemplated, which shall be available for inspection and copying by the Artist at reasonable times and upon reasonable notice during regular business hours in order to verify any statement or accounting rendered hereunder.

14. **(Name of Art Publishing Company)** shall account to the Artist within ninety (90) days following each June 30 and December 31 during the term hereof, each such accounting to be accompanied by that amount, if any, therein shown to be payable to the Artist.

15. This Agreement contains the entire understanding of the parties and shall be construed under and in accordance with the laws of the State of _____.

We, the undersigned, confirm that the foregoing accurately and completely sets forth our entire understanding by signing below.


_____

_____

(Name of Art Publishing Company Rep)     (Name     of Artist)


_____

_____

Date

**Introductory Licensing Letter**

Date

Name
Name of Company
Street Address
City, State, Zip

Dear _____ :

I'd like to introduce my line of art designs.  Some of the imagery suggests use in a number of product venues, especially **(product the company produces, i.e., plates, wall hangings, etcetera).**

I've enclosed several designs for your review.   There are additional designs at online at **(your website address)** and I invite you to preview those, as well.

I'm most interested in talking with you about licensing possibilities.  I appreciate your consideration of my work and I look forward to speaking with you.

 Sincerely,

## Sample Licensing Contract

*A word of caution*:  this sample licensing agreement is **NOT** presented as the perfect example of the instrument, nor as an industry standard.  If a potential client offers a contract that is composed in such a manner that the artist is unable to completely understand everything contained in it, consult an attorney.

Most of the companies that license imagery for use on their own products will have their own standard licensing contract.  It is up to the artist to read every word of that contract and make sure he understands exactly what rights he is signing away and what rights he is retaining.  When in doubt, consult an attorney.

And remember, a bad license is probably worse than no license.

### *Sample Licensing Agreement for Licensing Images to Users*

1.0 Parties
'The Licenser' (Name and address of the Artist)
'The Licensee' (Name and address of Client)

1.1 Definitions
1.1.1 'Artwork' means transparency, positive, negative, electronic scan, work of art, painting, montage, drawing, engraving, work of artistic craftsmanship, rough drawing or rough creations or any other representations of the Licensers property or any part thereof including any representation consisting of a recording or light or other radiation or electronic signal on any medium on which an image is produced or from which an image may by any means be produced including any film or storage in a computer and artistic merit shall not be any

consideration in determining what constitutes artwork.

1.1.2 'Net Receipts' all income accruing to the Licensee from the exploitation of the Rights as hereinafter defined excluding any vat payable thereon and after the deduction of all costs and charges and expenses properly and reasonably incurred in connection with their exploitation as set out in Schedule II of this Agreement or otherwise agreed in writing between the Licenser and the Licensee on a product by product basis.

1.1.3 'Licensers Property' the property of the licenser as notified in writing by the Licenser to the Licensee.

1.1.4 "Merchandised products' those products, designs and publications which use under the license all or part of the Artwork or images derived therefrom and referred to as the Subject Matter of this Agreement

1.1.5 'the Rights' the exclusive right by way of license for the Licenser to produce reproduce, publish sell and distribute and further to grant the non-exclusive right to the Licensee to manufacture package distribute market and sell or publish the Merchandised Product in the Territory

1.1.6 'the Territory' means the geographic areas as specified in Schedule II

2.0 Recitals: whereas (i) the Licenser is the exclusive agent for licensing the images and Artwork of the subject Matter specified in this agreement and has the right to enter into contracts with manufacturers and suppliers to manufacture or publish merchandising products under license incorporating imagery or artwork taken from and of the Subject Matter of this Agreement (ii) The Licensee is a manufacturer distributor designer or publisher of merchandised products incorporating the images or artwork of characters, picture, images and works of the original design.

2.1 Subject Mater: The Artwork as listed and particularized in Schedule I And herein referred to in this Agreement as the Subject Matter a reproduction of which is to be incorporated in Merchandised Products manufactured distributed or published by the Licensee.

2.2 Licensee: Under this agreement the Licensee shall have the non-exclusive, non-transferable, revocable right to manufacture distribute design or publish Merchandised Products based on and incorporating images of the Artwork being the Subject Matter of this agreement. This Agreement shall remain in force until Either all the Merchandised Products made or derived from the Subject Matter are sold whereupon a statement confirming all sales and receipts shall be supplied to the Licenser OR where the Licenser gives 6 months written notice of termination OR upon the expiry of the contracted period of the Agreement as specified on the invoice or in Schedule II

2.3 Consideration: The Licensee agrees to pay to the Licenser a fee as specified on the invoice and / or in Schedule II

2.4 Licensers Obligations: The Licenser warrants that it owns the license to the Rights to this Agreement and that it has the right to enter into this Agreement and that there is no present claim or litigation in respect of those Rights relating to the Subject Matter.

2.5 Licensee's Obligations: (i) The Licensee agrees that the Licenser shall in its absolute discretion be entitled to approve all material of the Artwork and Merchandised Product prior to production, manufacture and distribution and the Licensee acknowledges that such approval must be in writing. (ii) The Licensee confirms that a comprehensive public and product liability insurance policy is and will be in force covering any claims actions or damages which may arise as a direct or indirect result of the use by the public of the Merchandised Products. (iii) The Licensee undertakes that the Merchandised Products will not be offensive or obscene in nature or derogatory of any third party and will not expose the Licenser to civil or criminal proceedings. (iv) The Licensee will use its best endeavors to ensure that the Merchandised Products do not contain any material which infringes the copyright or design rights of any third party. (v) The Licensee acknowledges and agrees to ensure that all third parties to be contracted by the Licensee in respect of the Merchandised Products incorporating images of the Artwork will agree that all copyright and any other rights concerning the same together with any goodwill are and shall remain the sole property of the Licenser. (vi) The Licensee shall not sell or consign for sale any Merchandised Product outside the Territory unless with the prior written consent of the Licenser. (vii) The Licensee shall provide the Licenser with an annual audited statement recording complete accounting details of such of its income and expenditure as is relevant for the purpose for calculating the Licenser's receipts from this Agreement in such instances where payment is calculated on a royalty basis. (viii) The Licensee hereby unconditionally and irrevocably undertakes to indemnify the Licenser against all actions proceedings claims damages reasonable costs and losses whatsoever made against or incurred by the Licenser in consequence of any breach by the Licensee of any term of this agreement.

2.6 Quality and Design of Merchandised Product: The Licensee undertakes and agrees that the Merchandised Product shall be of a high standard and of such style appearance and quality as to be suited to exploitation to the best advantage of the Artwork and to protect and enhance the value of the Licenser's Property and the goodwill relating to it.

2.7 Promotional Material: The cost of promotional material and Artwork to be used by the Licensee in connection with the Merchandised Product shall be borne solely by the Licensee. The Licenser shall have the right but not the obligation to use the name of the Licensee in any publicity or advertising relating to the Merchandised Product.

2.8 Infringement: In the event of infringement of either the copyright or the Licenser's rights by any third party the Licensee will take all reasonable steps in assisting the Licenser to take such action as may in the Licenser's sole discretion be required to protect those rights.

2.9 Credits: The Licensee will ensure that the words " By Courtesy of The Art Business " or such other words and if appropriate the Licenser's logo as the Licenser shall direct shall be included on all Merchandised Products

2.10 Entire Agreement: This Agreement in conjunction with the Terms & Conditions of Submission and Reproduction of Images constitutes the entire understanding between the parties and supersedes any arrangements, understandings, promises or agreements made or existing between the parties prior to or simultaneously with this Agreements. No variation of this Agreement shall be effective unless it is in writing and signed by and on behalf of both parties.

2.11 Governing Law: This Agreement shall be governed by and construed in all respects in accordance with English Law.

3.0 Authorized signatures:
On behalf of the Licenser On behalf of the Licensee

Signed:
Title:
Date:

Signed:
Title:
Date:

4.0 Schedule I
A detailed description of the Artwork and the Image including any attributable name and the catalogue number and recording any form or reference or coding together with details of the ownership of copyright.

4.1 Schedule II
Calculation of fees payable including (i) Basic price and conditions (ii) Quantity Discount (iii) Authorized Use (iv) Territory (v) Period of Use (vi) Terms of non Exclusivity.

4.2 Schedule III
Any restrictions specifically required by the owner of the original image or copyright.

### Required Reference Material

*Artists & Graphic Designer's Market*

This annual publication lists on average some 4000-plus art buyers. This is the best place to start looking for clients to buy Fine Art, Illustration, Graphic Design and Cartoons.

This book is readily available at most any bookstore and retails for around $30.00 (USD).

*Advertisers Index*

This annual publication lists every advertiser in the United States that spends a minimum of $50,000 a year on advertising. This is the best place to start looking for clients for Licensing imagery, Product Design and Package Design. For the artist with an interest in specializing in Advertising Art, this volume is indispensable.

Specialty business books tend to be expensive due to a limited reading audience. This volume retails for around $1000.00 (USD), but the Business Section of most public libraries will have a Reference Copy on the shelf.

## Entrepreneurial Resources

### Sample Sales Package

The samples used in this section are my own.  They were chosen for several reasons, mainly because they were readily available.  They are not necessarily presented as the best possible examples of Sales material, but they have proven effective.

### Business Card

An art example is a nice addition to the card.  Color can be effective, but a properly designed black and white card works just as well.

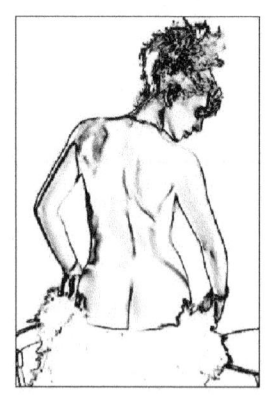

**Douglas Ready**
*Fine Art & Illustration*

2424 NW 59th Street #102
Seattle, Washington 98107

**206-933-8313**

www.douglasready.com

## Stationery

I've found it more effective not to print artwork on the stationery, instead allowing the business card to introduce artwork.

## Catalog Blank

A stationery template works very well for inserting product information.

## Catalog Page

Showcase your product, not your ad design abilities.

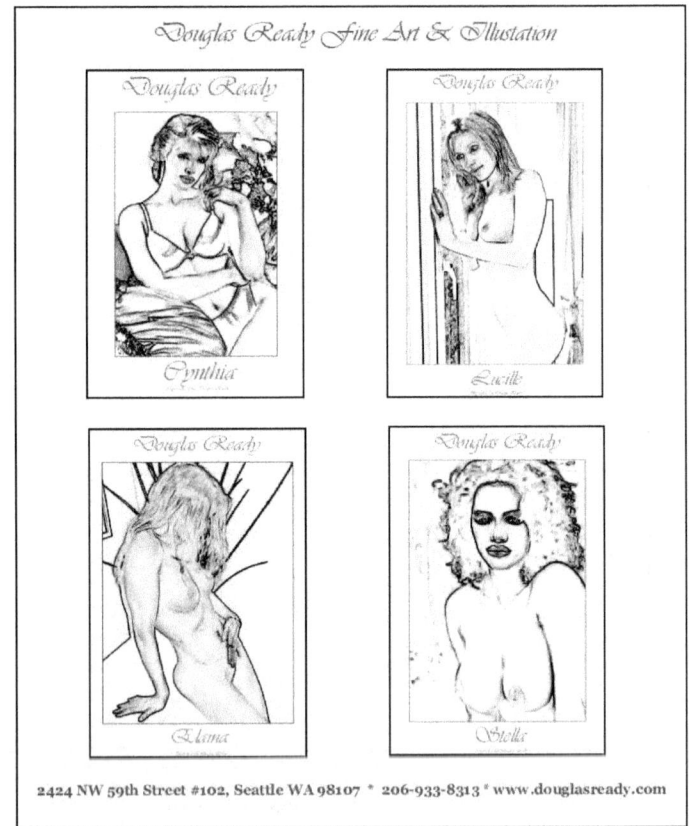

## Order Insert

This slips into a Catalog Blank template.

## Catalog Order Page

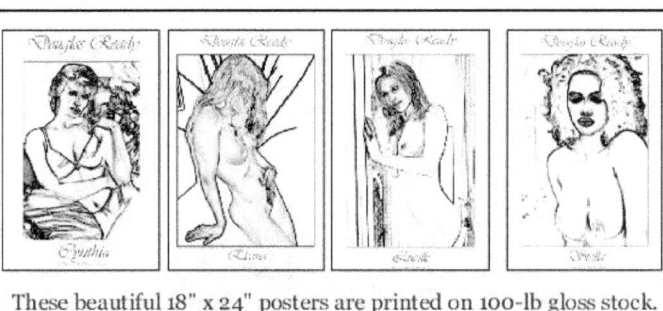

These beautiful 18" x 24" posters are printed on 100-lb gloss stock.
The Retail Price is $35.00 per poster.
The Minimum Wholesale Order is $175.00.

Cynthia _____ copies @ $17.50 each = $_____

Lucille _____ copies @ $17.50 each = $_____

Elaina _____ copies @ $17.50 each = $_____

Stella _____ copies @ $17.50 each = $_____

shipping & handling = $   7.50

Total Order = $_____

Please make checks payable to

**Douglas Ready**

**Showcard**

The Showcard I use is roughly 12" square and mounted on foam core for easy display on a portable easel. It's a great introduction tool at festivals or when signing new releases at a gallery.

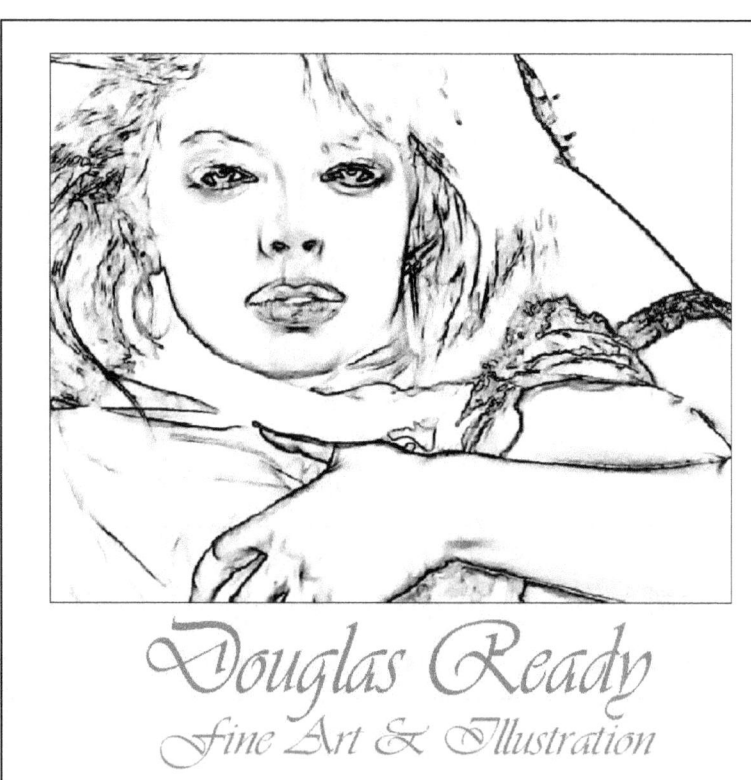

## Postcard

A postcard is an exceptionally effective mailer. The showcard design works well for this purpose.

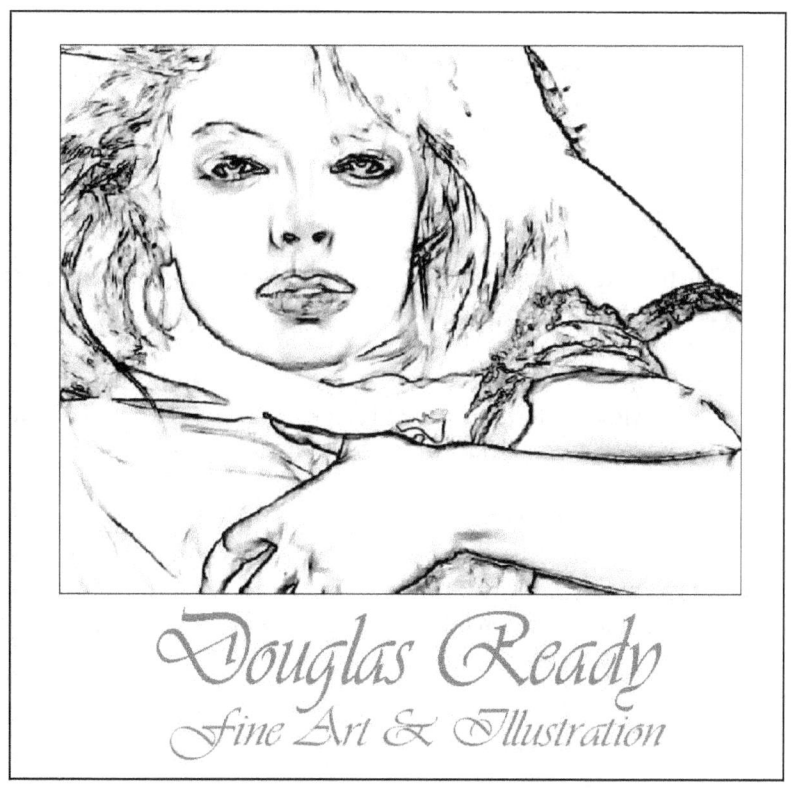

2424 NW 59th Street, Seattle, Washington 98107

*www.douglasready.com*

**Sample Sales Letter**

Date

Name
Name of Shop
Street Address
City, State, Zip

Dear _____ :

 I'd like to introduce my line of **(greeting cards, posters, etcetera)**.

I've enclosed a sample card and several promotional pieces for your review. There are more images available at my website and I invite you to visit the site at www.-----.com.

The suggested retail price per image is $_____.  I'm confident your customers will find the imagery appealing.

I appreciate your consideration of my work and I look forward to speaking with you.

 Sincerely,

### Telephone Sales Script

*You'll do much better putting your product into stores if you follow-up the Catalog mailing with a telephone call. This Script is geared toward a Greeting Card product, but is effective for any art product.*

**(Mr./Ms.) -----, my name is _____. I sent you a sample package of Greeting Cards about a week ago and I wondered if you'd had a chance to look at the package**?

(Respondent says NO, THE PACKAGE HASN'T BEEN REVIEWED)

> **I understand. I'd like to talk with you about the cards. What would be a good time for me to call you back?**
> (Make a note and call back.)

(Respondent says YES, THE PACKAGE HAS BEEN REVIEWED)

> **Did you like the cards?**

(Respondent says YES.)

> **Did any of the images stand out?**
>
> (Respondent says YES, ESPECIALLY...)
> **Can I assume you think the cards would do well in your shop?** (Direct the retailer to the order form, walk him through it, write up the order and fax or email a confirmation.)

(Respondent says NO, THE CARDS DIDN'T STRIKE HIM AS SOMETHING THAT WOULD WORK IN HIS SHOP.)

**I understand. If you don't mind my asking, what wasn't there that makes you feel the cards wouldn't be a good product for you to carry?**

(Listen and learn. There may be some validity to what the retailer has to say. If it becomes apparent that he simply doesn't care for the designs, thank him for his time and move on. If he's just wishy-washy, suggest trying a small order to see how the cards would do. Either way, thank the retailer.)

**Follow-up Sales Letter**

Date

Name
Name of Shop
Street Address
City, State, Zip

Dear _____ :

I'd like to thank you for  your  decision to carry my line of cards.

I'd be interested in any suggestions or observations from you concerning my product.   It's important that the line prove profitable for both of us.

I appreciate your consideration of my work and I look forward to working with you.

 Sincerely,

## Sample Retailer Application

If you're shipping product on a regular basis, it's a good idea to have this customer information on file. Generic applications can be found at any office supply store.

**Owner's Name/Address**

| Last: | First: | Country: | Phone: |
|---|---|---|---|
| Name of Business: | | | Fax: |
| Billing Address: | | | E-mail: |
| City: | State: | Zip: | Web: |
| Shipping Address (if not the same as billing): | | | |
| City: | State: | Zip: | Accounts Payable Contact: |

**Business Information** (a copy of your Business License or Tax ID must be included with application)

| Name of Principal responsible for Business: Last: | First: | Middle Initial: | Title: |
|---|---|---|---|
| Type of business: | Sole Proprietorship ☐ | Partnership ☐ | Corporation ☐ |
| Years in business: | Sales Tax ID: | | Resellers Permit Number: |

**Method of Payment** (New accounts are CIA or COD on all initial orders)

| Credit Card: ☐ MC, Visa | Check: ☐ | | C.O.D.: ☐ |
|---|---|---|---|
| Credit Card Number: | | Exp. Date: | |
| Name as it appears on Credit Card: | | | |
| Billing Address of Credit Card (if different from above) | | | |
| City: | State: | Zip: | |
| Authorized Signature: | | Date: | |

**Bank References** (complete only if applying for credit terms)

| Institution Name: | | Institution Name: | |
|---|---|---|---|
| Acct. Type    Checking ☐ | Savings ☐ | Acct. Type    Checking ☐ | Savings ☐ |
| Acct. # | | Acct. # | |
| Address: | | Address: | |
| Phone: | | Phone: | |

## New Accounts
- All new accounts must complete the Independent Retailer Application before orders can be shipped. Products are sold for the specific purpose of resale to the product's end user.

## Order Minimums
- Opening order minimum and re-order minimum is $150.00 USD.

## Payment Terms
- All invoices payable in United States Dollars to **(Your Company Name)**
- Payment due before shipment on all initial orders and accounts without established credit terms.
- Net 30 Terms apply to follow up orders.
- Re-orders will not be shipped to customers with unpaid past due balances.
- A $35.00 handling fee will be assessed for all returned checks at which time the account will be handled on a CIA only basis.

## Custom Orders
- Custom products are manufactured to order and are not returnable.
- Custom orders may not be cancelled if production has started.

## Warranty
- **(Your Company Name)** guarantees the products sold hereunder to be free from defects and material and workmanship.
- Warranty does not cover damage caused by normal wear and tear, abuse, misuse or accidents.
- Liability is solely limited to replacement product found by

**(Your Company Name)** to be defective.
- This warranty is in lieu of all other warranties, expressed or implied, in law or in in fact, including the warranties of merchantability and fitness for particular use.
- In no event, whether as a result of breach of contract or warranty will **(Your Company Name)** be liable for any incidental or consequential damages including, but not limited to, damages for loss of revenue, cost of capital, claims of retailer's customers for damages, and costs and expenses incurred in connection with labor, overhead, transportation, installation or removal of goods.

### Shipping
- Shipping charges are calculated individually per order and added to the invoice, based upon the weight and destination of order.
- All orders are accepted subject to delays due to strike, fire, flood, or other causes beyond our control.
- All orders are accepted without obligation on our part as to deliver date by carriers.

### Returns
- Returns are accepted for merchandise that is found to be defective, provided **(Your Company Name)** is notified within three (3) business days following delivery of said merchandise. Our liability is limited to replacement of said merchandise.

### Damage Claims
- All claims for damaged shipments must be made within three (3) days of receipt of good and unless so made will be consider void.
- Claims for loss or damage on collect shipment are the responsibility of the Customer to contact the freight carrier.

- Claims for loss or damage on prepaid shipments will be initiated by **(Your Company Name)** once notified by the customer of damage.
- Our products are carefully packaged and shipped in containers approved by transportation companies. We are not responsible for goods damaged by carriers.

### Acceptance, Successors and Assigns

- Orders are subject to final acceptance at the Corporate Office in **(Your Company Address)**.
- The rights, duties and obligation of Customer and **(Your Company Name)** shall be binding upon and inure to the benefit of their respective successors and legal representatives and may not be assigned in any manner without the prior written consent of the other party.

### Collections

- In the event that the Customer's account is sent to a commercial collection agency by **(Your Company Name)** for collection of past-due balances, the Customer is obligated to pay the balance due plus the billed collection fees including any attorney's fees and expenses incurred by **(Your Company Name)**.

### Law

The validity, interpretation and performance of these Terms & Conditions of Sale shall be governed by and construed in all respects in accordance with the laws of the State of Washington.

**I/WE authorize & direct all banks and credit reporting agencies to disclose to (Your Company Name) any and all information concerning the financial and credit history of my company and myself in order to seek credit terms.**

**I/We certify that all the information submitted on this form for the purpose of opening an account is true, correct and complete.**

**I/We fully understand and acknowledge by signing this document the Terms & Condition of Sale set forth by** (Your Company Name)**.**

_____

_____

Authorized Signature                                  Title

_____

_____

Printed                                           Name
Date

**Sample Sales Representative Agreement**

> *In dealing with independent Sales Representatives, I've found that most don't have contracts laying around their offices- -not surprising, since often those offices consist of a car and a briefcase.*
> *This letter confirming terms and requirements is a good way to keep everything straight.*

**Contact Person**
**Name of Sales Rep Firm**
**Street Address**
**City State Zip**

**Date**

Dear -----:

This is to confirm our conversation regarding Sales Representation of the **(Your Company Name)** Greeting Card product line by **(Name of Sales Rep Firm)** .

My understanding of our partnership terms are:

> **(Your Company Name)** will provide one **(or however many agreed upon)** complete Product Sample Kit to **(Name of Sales Rep Firm)** for the purpose of showcasing product to potential customers. The Sample Kit will contain one each of the entire **(Your Company Name)** line of Products, as well as **(Your Company**

**Name)** Promotional Items and Product Order Forms. New Product Samples will be provided to **(Name of Sales Rep Firm)** as they are released.

**(Your Company Name)** agrees to exclusive Sales Representation of our product line to retail stores in **(insert specific geographic area)** by **(Name of Sales Rep Firm)**. Retail Stores located within the specified geographic area that have an existing purchasing relationship with **(Your Company Name)** shall continue to deal directly with **(Your Company Name)** regarding product purchases and it is agreed that **(Name of Sales Rep Firm)** will not contact those Retail Stores for the purposes of selling **(Your Company Name)** product. **(Your Company Name)** will provide to **(Name of Sales Rep Firm)** a current list of **(Your Company Name)** Wholesale Customers located in the specified geographic area.

**(Your Company Name)** maintains a $150 Wholesale Order Minimum **(or whatever the amount is)**. Any orders placed which do not meet this Wholesale minimum will be billed at the regular Retail Price. **(Your Company Name)** agrees to ship complete order within five business days of receipt of the completed Order Form.

**(Your Company Name)** agrees to ship ordered merchandise directly to the customer and to provide verification of shipment to **(Name of Sales Rep Firm)**. **(Your Company Name)** will not accept returns on merchandise purchased at the Wholesale Price and all sales are final.

**(Your Company Name)** shall pay a commission of 20% **(or the amount agreed upon)** of the billed amount to **(Name of Sales Rep Firm)** on all orders generated by that firm. Commissions shall be paid within 30 days of receipt of payment to **(Your Company Name)** from the Wholesale Customer **(or whatever payment terms agreed upon)**.

**(Your Company Name)** will provide racks upon request to selected retailers / does not provide display racks to retail stores **(select one)**.

**(Your Company Name)** and **(Name of Sales Rep Firm)** enter into this partnership voluntarily, and partnership may be dissolved by either party by written notification.

In the event of dissolution, the total obligation of **(Your Company Name)** to **(Name of Sales Rep Firm)** shall be the payment of full commissions on orders received prior to the date of such written notification . **(Name of Sales Rep Firm)** agrees to return the full Sample Kit to **(Your Company Name)** within ten days of written notification should said partnership be dissolved.

I have enclosed two copies of this letter. Please sign one copy and return it to me at your earliest convenience.

If your understanding of the terms of our agreement differ from my understanding, please contact me immediately.

I look forward to a profitable working relationship with **(Name of Sales Rep Firm)**.


Sincerely,


_____

**(Your Name)**


_____

**(Your Company Name)**



_____

**(Name of Contact at Sales Rep Firm)**


_____

**(Name of Sales Rep Firm)**

## Greeting Card, Poster & Gift Distributors

There are any number of effective methods of identifying Wholesale Product Distributors.

Most distributors purchase listings in Trade Directories or Trade Journals--indeed, a number of Trade Journals actually publish an annual Vendor Directory Issue--and these volumes can be purchased at varying rates.

The Internet has proven itself a quick and enormously cost-effective method of identifying Wholesale Distributors. A query run through any large Search Engine will deliver dozens of bits of contact information.

As a courtesy to potential customers, a number of art publishers--especially greeting card and poster publishers--list directories of their Wholesale Distributors on the company website so that potential customers may more easily purchase company product.

At press time, the distributors listed here were deemed active and viable. These listings are in no way to be interpreted as an endorsement or recommendation of any of these firms or individuals. They are listed as a convenience for the budding art publishing entrepreneur as a place to begin the exploration process of identifying appropriate contracted representation.

**6 Bullfeathers Inc.,** 1558 Coshocton Ave 3216, Mt Vernon OH 43050
(740) 392-3855

**AirCo**, PO Box 562, Novato CA 94948
(415) 892-0808

**AJ & Associates**, 2052 Rainier Ave S, Seattle WA 98144
(206) 329-4321

**Arctic Circle, Inc.,** PO Box 956474 Duluth GA 30095
(770) 495-0222

**Artecnica, Inc.,** 3457 S. La Cienega Blvd. Building A, Los Angeles, CA 90016
(310) 559-3555

**A to Z Marketing**, 125 E Main St, Ste 7, Ripon CA 95366
(800) 814-1600

**Backyard Oaks**, 401 E. 8th Street Suite 310, Sioux Falls, SD 57103
(605) 338-1968

**Bad Monkey Productions**, 3530 SE Hawthorne Blvd #5, Portland OR 97214
(503) 232-9185

**Beauty & A Bee, Inc.,** 3839 Renate Dr, Las Vegas NV 89103
(702) 227-0080

**Beyond Wishes LLC**, 44 Sanchez St, San Francisco CA 94114
(415) 342-2935

**Birchcraft Studios**, P.O. Box 328, Rockland MA 02370
(800) 333-0405

**Bombshelle LLC**, 2256 N Albina, Ste 176, Portland OR
(971) 404-6079

**Card Cafe, Ltd**, 2321 Second Ave, Seattle WA 98121
(206) 269-0662

**CardExpress**, 1827 B. Hekla Ave, Winnipeg, Manitoba Canada 2R2 OK3
(800) 665-9021

**Card in the Box**, 350 S. Rohlwing Road, Suite 200, Addison, IL 60101
(630) 678-6408

**Carousel Greeting Cards, Inc.,** 704 Marshall St, Norristown PA 19401
(800) 355-2273

**Casey Group**, 16801 SE Newport Way, Issaquah WA 98027
(425) 747-9400

**Cavallini Papers & Co., Inc.,** 1630 17th Street, San Francisco, CA 94107
(415) 551-3590

**Cazier & Associates**, 17705 67th Place W, Lynnwood WA 98037
(425) 742-1978

**CCS Union Company**, 1186 S Van Ness Ave #2, San Francisco 94110
(415) 824-2973

**Consolidated Card & Supply, Inc.,** 3350 Emig Mill Rd, Dover PA 17315
(888) 774-3548

**Constance Kay, Inc.,** 5 Union Square West 6th Floor, New York, NY 10003
(646) 486-3250

**Cork Pops Inc.,** 7 Commercial Blvd, Novato CA 94949
(415) 884-6000

**Creative Imaginations**, 10879 Portal Dr, Ste B, Los  Alamitos 90720
(714) 995-2266

**CSD Enterprises**, PO Box 3489, San Leandro CA 94578
(510) 351-2840

**Delta C Enterprise, Inc.**, PO Box 612636, San Jose CA 95161-2636
(408) 321-9008

**Dyer Papiere**, Am Himmelfeld 19 Montabaur, D-56410 Germany
Toll-Free - 011492602947545

**E&M Specialty Company**, PO Box 3766, Sparks NV 89432
(775) 856-3131

**Enlightened Papers**, 618 NE Shaver Street Portland, OR 97212
(503) 284-7987

**Forum Novelties, Inc.,**  999 Gould St, New Hyde Park NY 11040
(516) 536-4600

**Frances Merchandise LLC,** 2707 Pastel Ave, Henderson NV 89074
(800) 747-5509

**Gift Connection**, Allentown PA 18109
(610) 435-5949

**Grateful Images**, 12335 Kingsride #181, Houston TX 77024
(713) 857-6265

**Heartland Greetings**, 1280 Albreton Place, Lebanon OH 45036
(513) 934-4328

**Hoff (Nikki)**, 3939 NE M L K BLVD, Portland OR 97212
(503) 287-7443

**Image Connection**, 456 Penn Street Yeadon, PA 19050
(800) 227-8178

**Inside Track**, PO Box 14665, Portland OR 97214
(503) 231-1248

**Johnson (Judy)**, 7500 SW Fulton Park Blvd, OR 97219
(503) 246-5707

**Laughing Elephant / Darling & Company**, 3645 Interlake Ave
N, Seattle WA 98103
(206) 447-9229

**Leanin Tree Inc.**, 6055 Longbow Dr, Boulder CO 80301
(303) 581-2153

**Lee and Associates**, Hyannis Port MA 02647
(508) 775-5556

**Loker & Associates**, West Redding CT 06896
(203) 938-3378

**Madison Park Greetings**, 1407 11th Avenue, Seattle, WA 98122
(800) 638-9622

**Majestic Greeting Cards, Inc.,** 6600 High Ridge Rd, Boynton Beach,                              FL                              33426
(800) 351-3515

**Maine Products Marketing,** Augusta ME 04333
(207) 624-7488

**Martin Associates,** 110 E 9th St, Ste C-1052, Los Angeles CA 90079
(800) 421-9434

**Mascot International**, 1055 Harriston St, Berkeley CA 94710
(510) 527-3965

**Milady Productions**, 5040 NE 41 St, Seattle WA 98105
(206) 524-4152

**Miller & Company**, 13321 127th Ave SE, Snohomish WA 98290
(360) 862-8750

**Molesh & Associates,** 13624 SE 180th St, Renton WA 98058
(425) 687-5941

**Monkey Business**, PO Box 80099, Portland OR
(503) 245-1435

**Morris Associates**, 20 Shadyside Ave, Summit, NJ 07901

(908) 522-1651

**Moss Marketing, Inc.,** 9418 Odin Way, Bothell WA 98011
(425) 483-3196

**Nareg International, Inc.,** 3661 San Fernando Rd, Glendale
CA 91204
(818) 500-8291

**Northern Lights Marketing,** #110-12251 No .2  Rd, Richmond
, BC V7E 2G3 Canada
(604) 272-7258

**Northpointe International**, 432 Constitution Ave, Camarillo
CA 93012
(805) 389-0087

**Northwest Reps**, PO Box 22410, Eugene OR 9742
(541)345-9424

**PARI**, PO Box  1164, San Mateo CA 94403
(650) 347-9511

**Peaceable Hill Paperie,** 424-A Main Street, Suite #5,
Ridgefield,                           CT                           06877
(203) 438-1863

**Pershnokov Company**, 3306 E. Terrace Seattle, WA 98122
(206)328-9136

**Porter & Associates**, 224 SW Dakota St, Portland OR 97239
(503) 226-6272

**Prestige Greetings LTD**, 328 Willis Avenue, Mineola NY 15501
(516) 294-1912

**Quality Lines & Associates**, 801 Walnut Drive, Oakley CA 94561
(925) 625-1387

**Ranger Miller Group**, 11706 44th Dr SE, Everett WA 98208
(425) 337-5816

**Reiss Associates**, 1250 17th St, San Fancisco 94107
(415) 863-0330

**Rentel Presents**, 1445 4th St, Berkeley CA 94710
(510) 527-1832

**Ruggles (Rick),** Washington DC 20007
(202) 944-5050

**Salazar (Rick),** 1459 18th St, San Francisco CA 94107
(415) 550-7464

**Salmon Bay Reps**, 25927 160th Ave SE, Kent WA 98042
(253) 639-1122

**Sebree & Associates**, 1511 Tanglewood Dr, Placerville CA 95667
(530) 621-2000

**Siegel (Barry),**3632 Black Feather Dr, El Sobrante CA 94803
(510) 222-5446

**Sha Cai Enterprises, Ltd**, #170 - 12420 No 1 Rd, Richmond, BC V7E 6N2 Canada
(604) 271-3880

**Shakti Blue**, 9040 SE Telford Rd, Boring OR 97009
(503) 663-9351

**SMC**, 1733 Balboa St, Eugene OR 97408
(541) 341-6411

**Smith-Western Company**, 2223 S 80th St, Tacoma WA 98409
(253) 671-2100

**Specialty Wholesale**, 35718 Knox Butte Rd, Albany OR 97321
(541) 924-0727

**Spectrum Marketing LLC**, Voorhees NJ 08043
(856) 751-6598

**Stephen Joseph, Inc**, 4302 Ironton, Lubbock TX 79407
(800) 725-4807

**Taku Graphics**, 5763 Glacier Hwy, Juneau AK 99801
(907) 780-6310

**Trends International**, 7555 N Woodland Dr, Indianapolis IN 46278
(317) 388-1212

**Tsukineko, Inc.**, 17640 NE 65th St, Redmond WA 98052
(425) 883-7733

## Suggested Reading

There are literally hundreds of published volumes available that might well prove useful. I've selected some I've found to be especially helpful.

*The Artist's Guide to New Markets: Opportunities to Show & Sell Art beyond Galleries* by Peggy Hadden

*Awaken the Giant Within* by Anthony Robbins

*The Basic Guide to Pricing Your Craftwork: With Profitable Strategies for Recordkeeping, Cutting Material Costs, Time and WorkPlace Management, Plus Tax* by James Dillehay

*A Basic Guide to Writing, Selling and Promoting Children's Books: Plus Information about Self-Publishing* by Betsy B. Lee

*Business and Legal Forms for Fine Artists* by Tad Crawford

*The Business of Being an Artist* by Daniel Grant

*The E-Myth* by Michael Gerber

*Getting The Word Out: The Artist's Guide to Self-Promotion* by the Editors Of Art Calendar

*Guerrilla Marketing Attack: New Strategies, Tactics & Weapons for Winning Big Profits from Your Small Business*

by Jay Conrad Levinson

*Guerrilla Selling: Unconventional Weapons & Tactics For Increasing Your Sales* by Jay Conrad Levinson, Bill Gallagher & Orvel Ray Wilson

*How to Break Into Product Design* by Pamela Williams

*How to Make Money as an Artist: The 7 Winning Strategies of Successful Fine Artists* by Sean Moore

*How to Master the Art of Selling* by Tom Hopkins

*How to Start a Faux Painting or Mural Business: A Guide to Earning Money in the Decorative Arts* by Rebecca Pittmen

*How to Succeed as a Lifestyle Entrepreneur: Running a Business Without Letting It Run Your Life* by Gary Schine

*How to Survive and Prosper as an Artist: Selling Yourself without Selling Your Soul* by Caroll Michels

*Legal Guide for the Visual Artist* by Tad Crawford

*The Martha Rules* by Martha Stewart

*The McGraw-Hill Guide to Starting Your Own Business: A Step-by-Step Blueprint for the First-Time Entrepreneur* by Stephen C. Harper

*New Tax Guide for Artists of Every Persuasion* by Peter Jason Riley & John Jason Riley

*Outnegotiate Your Competition* by Harvey Mackay

*The Secret Power Within: Zen Solutions to Real Problems* by Chuck Norris

*Self-Promotion for the Creative Person: Get the Word out about Who You Are and What You Do* by Lee T. Silber

*Small Business Accounting Simplified* by Daniel Sitarz & Dan Sitarz

*Small Time Operator: How to Start Your Own Business, Keep Your Books, Pay Your Taxes, and Stay Out of Trouble* by Bernard B. Kamoroff

*Start Your Own Crafts Business: Your Step-by-step Guide to Success* by Entrepreneur Press

*This Business of Art* by Diane Cochrane

*Ultimate Sales Letter: Boost Your Sales with Powerful Sales Letters, Based on Madison Avenue Techniques* by Daniel S. Kennedy

*Unlimited Power* by Anthony Robbins

*What No One Ever Tells You About Starting Your Own Business* by Jan Norman

*Writing and Illustrating Children's Books* by Berthe Amoss and Eric Suben

**Web Resources**

The following list is by no means complete. These

particular sites are recommended as starting points and inclusion in this list is not necessarily an endorsement by the author.

## ARTISTS ASSOCIATIONS
### American Watercolor Society
http://www.americanwatercolorsociety.org/
Artists association for those specializing in the use of watercolor.

### Association of Medical Illustrators
http://www.ami.org
A site for anyone interested in the highly specialized niche of medical illustration.

### Association of Science Fiction and Fantasy Artists
http://www.asfa-art.org/
ASFA was organized for artistic, literary, educational and charitable purposes concerning the visual arts of Science Fiction, Fantasy, Mythology and related topics.

### Cartoonists Association
http://www.cartoonistsassociation.com
A website for cartoonists built and maintained by cartoonists.

### Graphic Artists Guild
http://www.gag.org
Organizations, Publications & Websites for Art Professionals.

### Independent Greeting Card Professionals Association
http://groups.yahoo.com/group/GreetingCardProfessionals
An international organization of 700+ greeting card creators who self-publish and market their own products to retailers and wholesalers.

### National Oil and Acrylic Painters' Society
http://www.noaps.org/
Trade organization for professional artists.

### National Cartoonists Society
http://www.reuben.org
Home and birthplace of the famed Reuben Awards, this organization is the premiere professional cartoonist association.

### Society of Children's Book Writers & Illustrators
http://www.scbwi.org
SCBWI is the premier organization for professionals in children's publishing.

### The Society of Illustrators
http://www.societyillustrators.org
This organization works to promote the interest of professional illustrators. Information on exhibitions, career advice, and many other links provided.

### BUSINESS
### Art Business.com
http://www.artbusiness.com
Contains art business related articles, reviews on business of art books and sells classes on marketing for artists.

### Art Business News
http://www.artbusinessnews.com/
Art Business News is a trade publication for the gallery and interior-design retail markets.

**Artist Help Network**
http://www.artisthelpnetwork.com
Find career, legal, money advice along with multiple regional, national and international resources.

**EBay**
http://www.ebay.com/
An online auction site that offers the artist an opportunity to sell original art and products derived from the original art, such as prints and posters.

**Foreign Currency Converter**
http://finance.yahoo.com/currency?u
A simple to use international currency converter.

**The Greeting Card Association**
http://www.greetingcard.org/resources_links.html
Trade organization for the greeting card industry.

**QuickMBA**
http://www.quickmba.com/
A wide variety of pertinent business article on such subjects as Marketing, Business Law, Management and Operations.

**PayPal**
https://www.paypal.com/us/
Online payment service that allows you to accept credit cards and foreign currency, as well as receive cash payments by direct bank account transfer.

**Starving Artists Law**
http://www.starvingartistslaw.com.
Start here for answers to your legal questions.

### NetMBA
http://www.netmba.com/site/about/
International Center for Management and Business Administration site. Publishes pertinent online business articles on such subjects as Marketing, Accounting, Finance, Operations and Strategy.

### ProPay
http://propay.com
Online Credit Card Processor.

### SelfPromotion.com
http://www.selfpromotion.com/
SelfPromotion.com is the net's leading resource for do-it-yourself Web Promotion. Here you will find all the information and automatic submission tools you need to do the job quickly, efficiently, and most of all, properly. If you invest a little time into reading and using this resource, you'll not only do a much better job of promoting your site, but save yourself a lot of time and effort in the process. And best of all, it's FREE.

### Selling Your Art Online
http://1x.com/advisor/
SYAO is a newsletter that covers topics that artists and crafts people need to know to successfully sell their creative work on the Internet. This web site is an archive of past articles, resource links, and an extensive listing of online galleries created by subscribers to the Selling Your Art Online newsletter.

### Tera's Wish
http://www.teras-wish.com/marketing
Tera Leigh, author of *How to Be Creative If You Never Thought You Could* (North Light Books) shares tips and ideas for

marketing, promotion, P.R. and more.

## US Copyright Office
http://www.copyright.gov
United States Copyright Office. Download forms and file online.

## Wholesale Central
http://www.wholesalecentral.com/Party_Items_Greeting_Cards. html
The Internet's largest wholesale directory and marketplace of active Party Items & Greeting Cards wholesalers, importers, and manufacturers.

## PRIVATE LABEL MANUFACTURING
## Cafe Press
http://www.cafepress.com/cp/info/
Online marketplace where you can create sell made-to-order custom products from your artwork, such as posters and prints and various items of apparel.

## LuLu
http://www.lulu.com/themes/create/homepage.php
On demand book, calendar and image printer.

## Zazzle
http://www.zazzle.com/
Online marketplace where you can create sell made-to-order custom products from your artwork, such as posters and prints and various items of apparel.

## ILLUSTRATORS
### Colossal Directory of Children's Publishers
http://www.signaleader.com/childrens-writers/
A free online list of publishers who produce children's material--books and magazines--with contact information and submission guidelines for each individual publisher.

### Greetings, etc. Magazine
http://www.greetingsmagazine.com/greetings/index.shtml
Greetings etc. is the only trade magazine that exclusively covers the greeting card, stationery products and party goods markets.

### Illustration magazine
http://www.illustration-magazine.com/
Artists' magazine devoted to the art of illustration.

### Magatopia
http://www.magatopia.com
Online magazine articles, web searches for art jobs, weekly columns on freelancing.

### Writers Write:  Greeting Cards
http://www.writerswrite.com/greetingcards
This site has links for artists with greeting card companies and submission information.


## FINE ARTISTS
### Altpick
http://www.altpick.com
The Source for Creative Talent & Imagination: news, competition deadlines, artist listings and more.

### American Artist Magazine
http://www.myamericanartist.com/
American Artist - MyAmericanArtist.com provides advice, inspiration, and practical how-to's for both professional and aspiring artists.

### Art Deadlines List
http://www.artdeadlineslist.com
The e-mail version of this list is free. It's a great source for deadlines for calls for entries, competitions, scholarships, festivals and more.

### Art Dealers Association of America
http://www.artdealers.org
Opportunities and information on marketing your work, galleries and dealers.

### Art Deadline
http://www.artdeadline.com
Called the "Art Professionals Resource," this site lists information for funding, grants, commissions for art in public places, representation.

### The Artist Magazine
http://www.artistmagazine.com
Archives of articles covering everything from the newest type of colored pencil to techniques in watercolors.

### Artist Registry
http://www.artistregistry.com
A registry where you can post art, get updates on calls for entries throughout the United States and much more.

### The Artists Network

http://www.artistsnetwork.com
Get articles, excerpts and tips from The Artist Magazine, Watercolor Magic, and Decorative Artist's Workbook.

### Artline
http://www.artline.com
Art Line is comprised of seven dealer associations, Art Dealers Association of America, Art Dealers Association of Greater Washington, Association of International Photography Art Dealers, Chicago Art Dealers Association, International Fine Print Dealers Association, San Francisco Art Dealers Association, and Society of London Art Dealers. The website has information about exhibits and artists worldwide.

## PREMIER POSTER & PRINT PUBLISHERS
### Bruce McGaw Graphics
http://www.bmcgaw.com/
Bruce McGaw Graphics, has created a global publishing and distribution company that has become the world leader and trendsetter in the fine art poster and print industry.. Drawing work from both museum collections and McGaw exclusive artists makes this the largest selection in the industry.

### Leslie Levy Gallery
http://www.leslielevy.com/
Leslie Levy Fine Art has earned a reputation as one of the leading publishers of fine art posters. This publisher is unique in that it also offers the original art for sale online. Artists represented include Steve Hanks, Jamie Burnes, James Harrill and Peter Holbrook.

### Munson Graphics
http://www.munsongraphics.com/

Munson Graphics is a fine art publisher and distributor for posters, prints and stationery.

### Sundance Graphics
http://www.sundancegraphics.com/decorative-poster-distributor.asp
Poster publisher and distributor.

## CARTOONISTS & COMIC BOOK ARTISTS
### Animation Artist Magazine
http://www.animationartist.com
free daily animation news, animated reviews, animation articles, and previews of upcoming animated films & cartoons.

### Bud Plant, Inc
http://www.budplant.com/
Huge selection of comics, books on illustrators and more.

### Comic Book Resources
http://www.comicbookresources.com/
Comic Book Resources (CBR) is the leading comic book web site. Renowned for its high quality content and active community, CBR draws the most loyal audience of users. We serve over 600,000 unique fans every month. The site links to some 1700 comic book sites, including publishers, creators and fan sites.

### Creating Comics
http://www.members.shaw.ca/creatingcomics/index.htm
Creating Comics source of information for comic writers, artists, letterers, and self-publishers. Includes information on every aspect of comics creation, including an extensive section of the

process of self publishing.

### Diamond Distributors
http://www.diamondcomics.com/
The primary comic book distributor website. Includes the current catalog, as well as guidelines for submitting a book for distribution consideration.

## ADVERTISING, DESIGN & GRAPHIC ART
### Advertising Age
http://www.adage.com
This site is a database of advertising agencies.

### The Art Directors Club
http://www.adcny.org
Founded in 1920, this international not-far-profit organization features job listings, educational opportunities, annual awards in advertising, graphic design, new media and illustration.

### Communication Arts Magazine
http://www.commarts.com
Publication and website covering all aspects of creative pursuit from illustrators to designers to typography.

### ImageSite
http://www.imagesite.com
Searchable databases of advertising agencies, art reps, competitions, galleries and printers.

## MISCELLANIA
### Art Schools
http://www.artschools.com

A free online directory with a searchable database of art schools all over the world. They also have information on financial aid, majors and lots more.

### Artlex Art Dictionary
http://www.artlex.com
Art dictionary with more than 3,200 terms.

### Draw Magazine
http://www.drawmagazine.com/
subscriptions, back issues, etc.

### SQP Productions
http://www.sqpinc.com/
Specialty publisher site devoted almost exclusively devoted to pin-up art by some very good artists

## PRINTING & PACKAGING RESOURCES
### Bazzill Basics Wholesale Paper
http://www.bazzillbasics.com/
Wonderful colored cardstock, envelopes, and more!

### Big Posters, Inc
http://www.bigposters.com/indexo.html
Creative Juices Printing & Graphics Inc is a printing and graphics company with extensive knowledge and experience in full color digital printing, offset printing and screen printing.

### The Box Depot
ttp://www.theboxdepot.com
A huge variety of boxes for cards and other items.
*Canterbury Media Services, Inc*
http://www.cp-digital.com/fine_art_services.html

A corporate imaging center specializing in trade show graphics, displays, poster presentations and artist support services. Canterbury Media offers full service digital fine art printing to artists who need to create gallery-quality duplicates of original artwork or produce fine art originals from digitally created art.

### CatPrint
http://catprint.bz
Very quick, very reliable and very reasonably priced digital printing company.

### Cheap                              Card                              Stock
http://www.cheapcardstock.com/?promoid=20
This site sells cardstock in wide range of colors and textures.

### Clear Bags, Inc
http://www.clearbags.com/
Packaging supplier. Clear Bags are made of a superior acid-free and lignin-free material. At ClearBags.com you'll find an extensive variety of bags for retail packaging--mailers, envelopes and card stock and a variety of other materials.

### Digital Printing Company
http://digital printing company.com
Another digital printing resource.

### Giclee Print
http://gicleeprint.net
Giclee printing company.

### Golden Gate Litho
http://goldengatelitho.com/
Offers traditional and digital pre-press and specializes in printing small to medium–large runs as well as most finishing

needs.

### The Envelope Mall
http://www.envelopemall.com
Huge assortment of envelopes -- kraft, vellum, metallic etc.

### JakPrints, Inc
http://jakprints.com/home/index.php
Full color paper, apparel and sticker printing.

### Perfect Posters
http://perfectposters.com
Printer specializing in a variety of options for printing art in a poster format.

### Poster Printing, USA
http://posterprintingusa.com
Printer specializing in a variety of options for printing art in a poster format.

### PS Print
http://www.psprint.com/printing/index.asp
PsPrint.com offers the fastest average turnaround time and possibly the lowest price in the industry. The website features traceable customer interaction, instant pricing and ordering, real-time order status information, and online upload, preview and approval of artwork. When the job demands it, Ps Print can turnaround most orders in as little as one day.

### Uline
http://www.uline.com/
Shipping supply specialists--boxes, bubble wrap, shipping tubes, etcetera.

## COMPUTER SOFTWARE & ONLINE COMMUNITIES
### Doxdesk Parasite Checker
http://www.doxdesk.com/parasite/
A free site that will check your computer for adware. Simply go to the site and wait. The process takes less than five seconds.

### Google
http://www.doxdesk.com/parasite/
Premier Internet Search Engine that allows you to search for both websites and images.

### Serif Software
http://www.freeserifsoftware.com/
Serif is a software developer that focuses most of its marketing efforts on selling its products to be bundled into hardware. Serif offers these free software downloads to consumers:
> *PagePlus SE* - Desktop Publishing
> *PhotoPlus* - Photo and Image Editing
> *WebPlus* - Web Site Design & Publishing
> *DrawPlus* - Graphic Design and Vector Drawing
> *3DPlus* - 3D Animation and Modeling

### Wet Canvas
http://www.wetcanvas.com/
An online cyber community for artists working in any and all mediums.

## ARTISTS' MATERIALS
### Artists & Craftsman Supplies
http:// artistcraftsman.com

**Cheap Joe's Art Supplies**
http://www.cheapjoes.com/

**Daniel Smith Art Materials**
http://www.danielsmith.com/

**Dick Blick Art Material**
http://www.dickblick.com/

**Flax Art Supplies**
http:// flaxart.com

**Jerry's Artarama**
http://www.jerrysartarama.com/

**Madison Art Supplies**
http:// madisonartshop.com

**Meininger Art Supplies**
http:// meininger.com

**Mister Art**
http:// misterart.com

**Rex Art**
http://www.rexart.com/

## About the Author

Douglas Ready an artist, illustrator, cartoonist, author and entrepreneur living and working in Seattle, Washington, USA.

Doug's illustration work has been used in advertising, book illustration, greeting cards, posters, t-shirt designs, and coloring books. His cartoons have appeared in a variety of magazines. Doug has also done product design work--plush toys and puppets, puzzles, and consumer paper products (paper plates, napkins, party favors, etcetera).

Doug's created several alternative comic books and had two runs at national syndication of a comic strip. He has taught cartooning in a number of venues, including a course at the University of South Carolina.

Doug recently formed **DMR Creative Enterprises** to publish and market his self-directed efforts under the label **Serendipity Press**. He is a former partner in **Carousel Studios** and the former owner of **Studio 5 Design**, which specialized in greeting card and poster publishing.

Doug is currently working on a graphic novel. His popular webcomic **Beach Drive** can be found online at www.douglasready.com.